Technology-Based Learning

A HANDBOOK FOR TEACHERS AND TECHNOLOGY LEADERS

Technology-Based Learning

A HANDBOOK FOR TEACHERS AND TECHNOLOGY LEADERS

REVISED EDITION

by

Tweed Wallis Ross, Jr.

and

Gerald D. Bailey

IRI SkyLight

TRAINING AND PUBLISHING, INC.

Arlington Heights, Illinois

Technology-Based Learning:
A Handbook for Teachers and Technology Leaders (Revised Edition)
First Printing

Published by IRI/SkyLight Training and Publishing, Inc.
2626 S. Clearbrook Dr., Arlington Heights, IL 60005
800-348-4474 or 847-290-6600
FAX 847-290-6609
info@iriskylight.com
http://www.iriskylight.com

Creative Director: Robin Fogarty
Managing Editor: T. B. Zaban
Editor: Michael Carpenter
Proofreader: Edward Roberts
Cover and Illustration Designer: David Stockman
Formatters: Dave Glick, Linda Glick, Bruce Leckie, Heidi Ray
Production Supervisor: Bob Crump

LCCCN 96-78481
ISBN 1-57517-074-4

1919-10-96V
Item Number 1468

CONTENTS

PREFACE TO THE SECOND EDITION

American education is undergoing serious redesign, and Americans are rethinking the role of schools and how children learn. Many experts assert that technology plays an increasingly important role in this effort to improve educational practices in preparation for the next century. An integral part of these efforts involves computers, networks, laser disks, modems, fax machines, television, VCRs—in short, a whole host of electronic gadgetry in the classroom. This dizzying array of advanced technology has left teachers bewildered both about how this "stuff" can be used to enhance traditional educational practices and how it can contribute to the development of new practices. This book addresses these concerns in ways which invoke the minimum of educational jargon, theory, and technical expertise.

Every year, teachers are required to attend workshops on technology topics or district-hosted in-service activities that introduce them to the latest technical marvel of the Internet, multimedia, computer networking, or electronic learning systems. They come away from these activities wondering how these combinations of software and hardware can be used to enhance the educational opportunities of students. What would make the additional effort and expense of purchasing, learning, and using these technologies worthwhile, compared to the ways of teaching they have been using?

This book was written to help them with just this sort of problem. Realistically, quality education is dependent on quality teachers using quality tools. This book presents education using new electronic technology in a frame of reference that isolates these technologies into five technology-based learning methods. Teachers adopt the technology-based learning method that best suits their classroom needs and incorporate the technology that will enhance their chosen methodology. Once teachers have focused on the methodology they wish to employ, this text gives them a general outline of what it will take to incorporate that methodology and what they can reasonably expect from their students once they incorporate it.

Each technology-based learning method is accompanied by a series of tips, tricks, and traps that help in its implementation in the classroom. Further, a series of resources providing a starting point for teachers in search of an effective technology is included.

Finally, the book provides an adoption model for incorporating technology-based learning methods into the school program. This model is useful for teachers in that it identifies specific activities that must be accomplished to insure the successful use of these learning methods in the classroom.

Teachers need resources to become the technology leaders they must become if information technologies are going to be incorporated into the classroom. This book is designed to help them become both: effective classroom teachers in the next century and technology leaders today.

◆

ACKNOWLEDGMENTS

In writing this book, the authors have incurred the debt of a legion of friends. The errors and omissions remain with the authors, but much of the substance of the book comes from the diligent work of a large number of practitioners in the field of education. These practitioners willingly donated their time and expertise. Through their thorough review and many helpful comments, the principals, educators, and technology specialists who aided in the field test of this handbook added much to the content.

We wish to thank our colleagues and fellow collaborators at Kansas State University. Their support and encouragement has been unflagging. Without their insight and intuition this handbook would never have come to print.

As always, our professional debt is to our closest colleagues, who are also our wives— Maxine and Gwen. Without their support, decency, rationality, and encouragement, publication would be a task whose burdens were far beyond the emotional rewards.

Finally, a special note of thanks is reserved for Dr. Gwen Bailey. Her tireless proofreading efforts hammered this document into a manageable form. Dr. Bailey's efforts in correcting both trivial and substantive errors is incalculable.

Tweed W. Ross and Gerald D. Bailey
September 1996

INTRODUCTION

KEY QUESTION

Why this handbook?

Educators at all levels are challenged to be agents of educational change. They find time, energy, and commitment stretched to unreasonable limits. American educational practices have placed heavy burdens on teachers in a time when classroom instructors are swimming in a sea of demands for change. This sea of demands seethes with calls for reform, restructuring, and transformation. Central to many of these change efforts are emerging technologies. Educators find it difficult to muster the energy and time to grasp new learning patterns generated by emerging technologies. This book provides all our friends in education a framework for using technology to enhance student learning.

Teachers need a definition of reform, restructuring, and transformation. In the general sense, "restructuring asks individuals at all levels of the educational system to change the way they think about and do their jobs" (David 1991, 39). This handbook focuses on the technology-based learning methods. Current change efforts differ from earlier attempts in two ways: 1) they are driven by challenging goals for student learning and 2) they call for systemic change of the educational system at all levels (David 1991). To that extent, this principal's handbook recognizes that technology is not the only factor involved in educational change. However, technology is a core aspect of educational change. Without making effective use of emerging technologies in the learning process, change efforts will be incomplete.

KEY QUESTION

What does this handbook do for teachers?

The purpose of this handbook is to give classroom teachers a working document that allows them to be leaders in creating technology-based learning methods. Often, when dealing with emerging technologies in the educational process, educators are left with puzzling questions.

"What are we planning for?"

"Where is all this leading to?"

"Where does it all fit in the school business?"

"What am I getting in to?"

This handbook frames answers to these questions. The handbook is designed for educators who are interested in using technology to alter their school's educational process **but** are neither experts, nor wish to become experts in technology. Often, technology planning activities provide the means without establishing the goals for new methods of instruction. *Technology-Based Learning* helps educators define the goals of technology planning efforts. This handbook also responds to the needs of technology experts who are creating new ways to use educational technology to enhance the learning process. This handbook empowers technology leaders in seven specific ways:

- This handbook provides background for understanding the principal's role in changing to Information-Age learning.

- This handbook provides a model for developing and adopting new technology-based learning methods.

- This handbook provides resources to use in developing and explaining new technology-based learning methods.

- This handbook provides technology leaders with information that helps frame their role in changing environments while furnishing resources and models for understanding technology's role in the rapidly changing learning process.

- This handbook provides goals for technology planning efforts.

- This handbook provides limited recommendations for specific brands without being committed to a particular platform or corporation.

- This handbook enables those charged with technology leadership to communicate learning goals with network administrators, software engineers, technicians, or technology coordinators.

In summary, this handbook helps technology leaders exercise a leadership role in implementing technology-based learning methods in their schools.

KEY DEFINITIONS:

Certain terms used throughout this book are crucial to a conceptual understanding of our meaning. Other authors may use different denotations, but these key definitions have been inserted here to establish clarity for the readers as they examine the text. Readers must grasp these definitions to understand our categorization of technology-based learning methods.

EMERGING TECHNOLOGIES

Emerging technologies are a general class of electronic learning tools, usually based on digital technologies, which are having a major impact on information manipulation, distribution and communication. These technologies include LCD panels, micro-computers, computer networks, television, modems, video-disc, CD-ROM, satellite, software, etc.

BUILDING PRINCIPAL

Building principal refers to individuals charged with the educational curriculum, building administration, instructional staff supervision, and organizational leadership of a school building.

SCHOOL REFORM

School reform refers to modifying schools in modest ways, such as raising standards, lengthening the school year, and establishing more stringent graduation requirements [see National Commission on Excellence in Education (1983) for examples of school reform].

SCHOOL RESTRUCTURING

School restructuring refers to substantial change in the educational process, such as site-based management, flexible time schedules, exhibitions of performance for graduation, and integrated courses [see Sizer, T., (1992c). *Horace's School* for an example of school restructuring].

SCHOOL TRANSFORMATION

School transformation refers to radically modifying the form and substance of education by reinterpreting teaching, learning, and knowledge. Teachers become guides. Learners become creators. Knowledge becomes a process of information literacy [see Papert, S. (1980). *Mind Storms;* S. Papert (1993). *The children's machine: Rethinking schools in the age of computers;* or Perelman, L. J. (1992). *School's out,* for examples of school transformation].

SYSTEMIC CHANGE

Systemic change ". . . is more complex and of wider scope, akin to redesigning a system; it alters roles, routines, and relationships within an organization" (David 1989, 52). Systemic change is analogous to the transition to learning organizations implied by Peter Senge in *The Fifth Discipline,* (1990) and second order change outlined by Larry Cuban in *The Managerial Imperative* (1988).

TECHNOLOGY LEADER

Those individuals associated with the educational system who, either through assigned role or assumed position, have achieved a position of prominence in the planning and implementation of electronic technologies at either the building or district level.

PART I

Background
Information
for
Technology
Leaders

CHAPTER 1

How to Use This Handbook

This chapter provides basic directions on how technology leaders can use this handbook to establish technology-based learning in their schools.

KEY QUESTION

What are the main parts of this handbook?

This handbook is designed as a resource book for educators and technology leaders seeking to use emerging technologies to alter learning programs. This handbook is not designed to be read in a linear, cover-to-cover fashion. It is designed so the reader can access information in any order. (See Fig. 1—Handbook Process, page 10.) At the end of each chapter is a list of suggested readings.

PART I

BACKGROUND FOR TECHNOLOGY LEADERS

This section outlines the educator's role in the changing paradigm caused by information technologies. PART I is required reading for educators seeking background information supporting change in learning practices caused by emerging technologies. Chapter Two outlines the changed paradigm of education and society. Chapter Three identifies the role of educational change leader.

PART II

TECHNOLOGY LEARNING METHODS

This section provides a model for understanding new technology-based learning methods. This model is based on the center of control for the learning process. The first chapter of this section should be read by all technology leaders who want to grasp the overall pattern of the subsequent five chapters. The subsequent chapters of this section, the five technology learning methods, can be investigated in any order.

PART III

TECHNOLOGY ADOPTION MODEL

This section contains two chapters. The first of these chapters is a Technology Adoption Model that provides a flowchart and checklist for technology leaders to use when adopting specific technology-based learning methods. This narrative should be read as a brief planning outline to begin implementation of chosen technology-based learning methods.

The second chapter, Professional Development, is an introduction to the often over-looked or underfunded aspect of technology adoption—staff development. Entire books have been devoted to this topic. However brief the treatment of staff development is in this book, effective technology leaders aggressively pursue resources strategies for the development of their staffs.

PART IV

RESOURCES FOR TECHNOLOGY ADOPTION

The final section is a collection of resources that educators can use as they develop programs and work with stakeholders on technology learning plans. Resources included in this section are a glossary, transparencies, a list of vendors, checklists, and a bibliography.

KEY QUESTION

What are the five steps to using this handbook?

STEP 1

Read Chapter 1 for background material on how to use this handbook.

STEP 2

Read Chapters 2 and 3 for material covering the change in education and society from an Industrial Era to an Information Age and how the role of the building principal has changed.

STEP 3

Read Chapter 4 to understand how the Technology-Based Learning Model (TLM) is used in this handbook.

STEP 4

Select a technology-based learning method to investigate. If the stakeholders feel a method has merit, go to step 5. If a method is unsuitable for this building or district, repeat step 4 and select another method for investigation.

STEP 5

Use the flowchart in Chapter 10 and other technology planning materials to implement the chosen technology-based learning method. Read Chapter 11 for a brief introduction into sound staff development practices to insure technological integration.

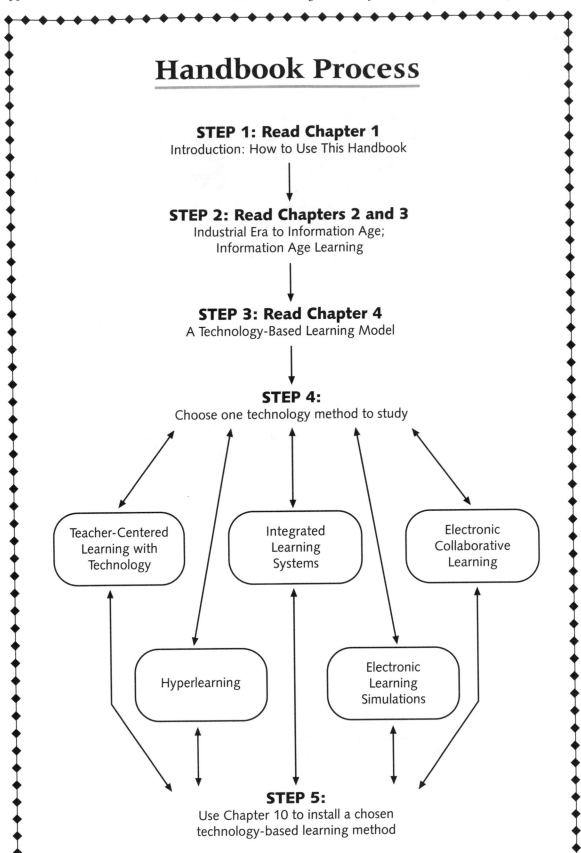

Handbook Process

STEP 1: Read Chapter 1
Introduction: How to Use This Handbook

STEP 2: Read Chapters 2 and 3
Industrial Era to Information Age;
Information Age Learning

STEP 3: Read Chapter 4
A Technology-Based Learning Model

STEP 4:
Choose one technology method to study

Teacher-Centered Learning with Technology

Integrated Learning Systems

Electronic Collaborative Learning

Hyperlearning

Electronic Learning Simulations

STEP 5:
Use Chapter 10 to install a chosen
technology-based learning method

Figure 1

IRI/SkyLight Training and Publishing

CHAPTER 2

Industrial Era to Information Age

*This chapter provides background
information on how technologies are
changing schools and society.*

KEY QUESTION

How are changes in the non-academic world impacting schools?

Currently, America is in the middle of an era of educational upheaval. During this era, many assumptions and practices of schooling are being challenged. This educational change effort is fueled by a paradigm shift (Barker 1992; Kuhn 1962) from an Industrial Age to an Information Age (McCarthy 1991; Nadler & Hibino 1990; Naisbitt & Aburdene 1990; Toffler 1990). This paradigm shift is fundamental to understanding current school change efforts.

This paradigm shift from an Industrial to an Information society should have urged schools to speed reforms of educational programs. Often it has not. Paralleling this paradigm shift from an Industrial to an Information Age are calls for fundamental educational change (Daggett 1989; Deming 1986; National Education Goals Panel 1991; Perelman 1992; Reich 1991; U.S. Department of Labor 1991). The world is changing "quickly, deeply and widely," but schools have been slow to recognize and react to these changes (White 1987, 41).

One hope for successful school restructuring in this maelstrom of change has been emerging technologies. While there has been some debate about the role of technology in student learning, there has been widespread anticipation that electronic learning methods provide a path around current unsuccessful change efforts (Bell & Elmquist 1992; Bruder 1990; Cawelti 1991; Collins 1991; Cuban 1992; Gibbon 1987; Jancich 1991; Mecklenberger 1990; Papert 1984; Pearlman 1991; Perelman 1989, 1990 & 1990a; Scheingold 1991). Emerging technologies have provided strong links for acquainting students with learning skills needed to survive in the Information Age (Johnston 1985; Newhard 1987; U. S. Congress Office of Technology Assessment 1988 & 1995; White 1987 & 1991). At the core of these educational change efforts are emerging technologies. These emerging technologies challenge many fundamental assumptions of education.

CHAPTER 3

Information Age Learning

*This chapter provides a brief description
of the educational change leader in an
Information Age school. Also, this chapter
provides a three-part framework for
using emerging technologies in the
learning process.*

KEY QUESTION

What is the role of the building principal in an Information Age school?

If emerging technologies provide the means for successful school restructuring, principals provide the operational guidance and leadership. Building principals lay the foundations and are the catalysts of school change. The principalship role is crucial for leading substantial change in public school settings. Lezotte (1990) outlined instructional leadership by principals as one of the correlates of effective schools. Fullan and Stiegelbauer (1991) emphasized the role of building principals as agents of change. English and Hill (1990) put principals at the "apex" of restructuring efforts. In short, principals are key players in the educational change process. The effort to prepare schools and students for the Information-Age demands technological leadership from principals.

To build new schools, principals must have (1) a vision of the new educational structure and (2) sufficient understanding of the construction techniques to enable them to use the technical skills of those they employ to carry out the vision. Technology and learning in the classroom are core components of the repertoire of skills necessary for principals to bring about educational change. (Ray 1992; Scheingold 1991). To provide a systemically changed educational environment, principals must orchestrate the integration of technology with new classroom learning strategies. If technology delivers real hope for changing schools, and principals are key players in this effort, building principals must understand teaching and learning in new technology-based classroom environments.

KEY QUESTION

What is the role of teachers in an Information Age school?

Fullan noted that principals play a gatekeeper, leadership role in any change activity involving public schools (1981). Systems thinking (Senge 1990) coupled with much of the effective schools research highlights the role of classroom teachers as leaders of change in schools. No single activity in the public highlights this phenomenon more than the implementation of instructional technologies. Teachers have more contact and more recent experience with new instructional technology. They understand its potential to alter learning methods in ways that are closely connected to classroom activities. Teachers cannot sit back and expect the administration to take the lead in developing new learning methodologies with emerging technologies. It may well be that administration provides resources, leadership, and bureaucratic experience to implement change. Classroom teachers provide the classroom experience, vision and dedication which allow these technologies to flourish in children's education. Implementing educational technology in the classroom is the role of both administration and teachers. Without either, educational change will not take place in the public schools. Principals must bring their teachers along and teachers must educate, inform, and support principals who are implementing technology change.

KEY QUESTION

How can leaders develop vision for integrating technology and learning?

Educational leaders understand Information Age technology-based learning methods better if they use three views to categorize teaching with emerging technologies. These three views are 1) teaching with technology, 2) teaching about technology, and 3) empowering with technology.

VIEW A

TEACHING WITH TECHNOLOGY

In View A, traditional subject matter is presented in new and exciting ways by instructors skilled in using the emerging educational technologies. This view fits well with the Effective Schools movement. In teaching with technology, instructors use technology to enhance and monitor student learning. **Technology is a tool.** (See Transparency. Intro.-1a and 1b to explain this concept.)

VIEW B

TEACHING ABOUT TECHNOLOGY

In View B, instruction is seen as a process to enable students to compete successfully in a highly technical work world. Students are taught thinking, manipulative, and process skills that enable them to become effective employees in a world dominated by high technology. Willard Daggett (1989) and the SCANS Report (1991) outlined fundamental technical skills students must acquire to be successful in the world of work. **Technology is a subject.** (See Transparency. Intro.-2a and 2b to explain this concept.)

VIEW C

EMPOWERING WITH TECHNOLOGY

In View C, educational technology becomes an empowering process. This view has been advocated by numerous scholars and educators. Empowering with technology is the process where the art of teaching changes from "sage-on-the-stage" to "guide-on-the-side." Learning becomes saturated with technology. Students become self-directed learners. They learn and study in "technology infused environments" (Papert 1980). Their investigations fulfill or expand their own constructionist meanings. Papert (1980), Marshall McLuhan (1964), Ted Nelson (1987), Christopher Dede (1987), Robert Reich (1991) and Alan Kay (1991) have supported the concept of empowering with technology. In this empowered environment, learning takes place in a world of information literacy where "anyone, learns anything, anytime, anywhere." **Technology is empowering.**(See Transparency. Intro.-3a and 3b to explain this concept.)

In summary, the Information Age and emerging technologies have had a great impact on education. Technology leaders of developing programs and practices for schools must prepare students for a changed world. To do this they must understand how these technologies apply to the learning process. Teachers must have a vision of the role of technology in education. The next section applies a vision to five selected methods for directing learning with technology.

Recommended Readings for PART 1, Background Information

Bailey, G. D., and G. L. Bailey. 1994. *101 Activities for creating effective technology staff development programs: A book of games, stories, role playing and learning exercises for administrators.* New York: Scholastic.

Bailey, G. D., and D. Lumley. 1993. *Technology staff development programs: A leadership sourcebook for school administrators.* New York: Scholastic.

Barker, J. A. 1992. *Future edge: Discovering the new paradigms of success.* New York: William Morrow and Co.

Cetron, M., and M. Gayle. 1991. *Educational renaissance: Our schools at the turn of the 21st century.* New York: St. Martin's Press.

Fullan, M. G., and S. Stigelbauer. 1991. *The new meaning of educational change.* New York: Teachers College Press.

Gardner, H. 1985. *Frames of mind: The theory of multiple intelligences.* New York: Basic Books.

McLuhan, M. 1962. *The Gutenberg galaxy: The making of typographic man.* Toronto: University of Toronto Press.

Mecklenberger, J. A. 1990. The new revolution. Special reprint from *Business Week No. 3191:* 22–26.

Nadler, G., and S. Hibino. 1990. *Breakthrough thinking: Why we must change the way we solve problems, and the seven principles to achieve this.* Rocklin, CA: Prima Publishing.

Papert, S. 1980. *Mindstorms: Children, computers, and powerful ideas.* New York: Basic Books, Inc.

————. 1984. New theories for new learning. *School Psychology Review, 13*(4): 422–28.

Perelman, L. J. 1992. *School's out: Hyperlearning, the new technology, and the end of education.* New York: William Morrow and Company.

Office of Technology Assessment. 1988. *Power on! New tools for teaching and learning.* Washington, DC: U. S. Government Printing Office.

————. 1995. *Teachers & technology: Making the connection.* Washington, D. C.: U.S. Government Printing Office.

Reich, R. B. 1991. *The work of nations: Preparing ourselves for 21st century capitalism.* New York: Alfred A. Knopf.

Scheingold, K., and M. S. Tucker, eds. 1990. *Restructuring for learning with technology.* New York: Center for Technology in Education and the National Center on Education and the Economy.

Toffler, A. 1990. *Power shift: Knowledge, wealth and violence at the edge of the 21st century.* New York: Bantum Books.

U. S. Department of Labor. Secretary's Commission on Achieving Necessary Skills. 1991. *What work requires of schools: A SCANS report on America 2000*. Washington, DC: U. S. Government Printing Office.

White, M. A., ed. 1983. *The future of electronic learning*. Hillsdale, NJ: Lawrence Erlbaum Associates

——, ed. 1987. *What curriculum for the information age?* Hillsdale, NJ: Lawrence Erlbaum Associates.

PART II

Technology-Based Learning Methods

CHAPTER 4

A Technology-Based Learning Model

This chapter provides a model for technology leaders to conceptualize new learning methods using emerging technologies. Five technology-based learning methods are provided.

KEY QUESTION:

Is there a model to help conceptualize learning in the Information Age?

Teachers need models to conceptualize emerging educational technologies within the overall framework of school change. This handbook provides a model based on five technology-based learning methods; each method is built on the concept of **learner control**. This model focuses on learning and technology's role in the learning process. This model does not relegate technology to the background of instruction, but centralizes technology in the learning process.

LEARNER CONTROL

The learner and the center of learning control are the essential features of this model. As part of the paradigm shift from the Industrial-Age to Information-Age schooling, this model investigates education **not** from an instructional, teacher, front of the classroom perspective; but from a learner, student, back of the classroom perspective.

The five technology-based learning methods outlined by this model inevitably become complicated since each one is bound up with every other. One method cannot be described without calling all other methods into consideration. **However, it is convenient at this time to separate this model into five methods as though they were unrelated.**[1]
Learner control is a critical component of the educational process. Traditional instructional practice has the teacher as the sole focus of learning. Teachers instruct as a "sages-on-the-stage." As the center for learner control changes from the sole teacher to many centers of learning, the role of the teacher changes to that of an aide, coach, motivator, facilitator, questioner, or "guide-on-the-side." Teachers' roles change change from examining the instructional process to examining the learning process. The five methods outlined in this model are based on a change in the control of the learning process brought about by emerging technologies.
School change surrounds the core of technology-based learning methods. The core efforts of technology-based learning methods are grouped in overlapping circles. (See Fig 2—Technology-Based Learning Methods) Each circle represents a central learning methodology using emerging technologies. They are Teacher-Centered Learning with Technology, Integrated Learning Systems, Electronic Collaborative Learning, Hyperlearning, and Electronic Learning Simulations.

Technology-Based Learning Methods

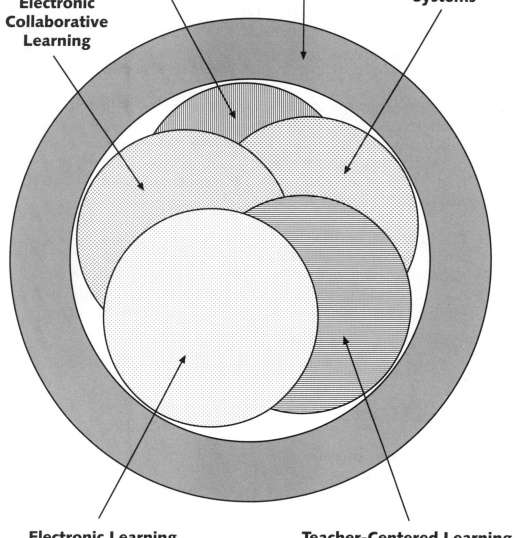

SCHOOL CHANGE EFFORTS

Hyperlearning

Integrated Learning Systems

Electronic Collaborative Learning

Electronic Learning Simulations

Teacher-Centered Learning with Technology

Figure 2

IRI/SkyLight Training and Publishing

- **TEACHER-CENTERED LEARNING WITH TECHNOLOGY.** Teacher-centered learning uses electronic technologies to provide instruction in traditional linear fashion: lecture, recitation, directed questioning. The teacher is in charge of the pace of instruction and the subject matter.

- **INTEGRATED LEARNING SYSTEMS.** Integrated Learning Systems (ILS) allow for accomplishment of specific learning outcomes through the use of computer technologies. **The machine, with a measure of teacher input, through highly structured, programmed administrative software, is in charge of the pace of instruction and the subject matter.**

- **ELECTRONIC COLLABORATIVE LEARNING.** Electronic collaborative learning uses emerging technologies for collaboration and cooperation among learners who may be separated by time or distance. **The collaborative team is in charge of the pace and direction of learning.**

- **HYPERLEARNING.** Hyperlearning (Perelman 1992) is an organizing principle recognizing the multidimensional fabric of knowledge linked with all its intellectual antecedents. Hyperlearning allows learners to follow preferences and control their own learning (Bevilacqua 1989). **The learner is in charge of the pace, order and depth of instruction, and subject matter.**

- **ELECTRONIC LEARNING SIMULATIONS.** Electronic learning simulations create environments for learning through electronic technologies. With this method students explore electronically created worlds. **The electronic simulation, with a strong measure of learner input, is in charge of the pace of instruction and the subject matter.**

KEY QUESTION

What are the features of each Technology-Based Learning Method?

This five-part technology learning model has several features that need to be recognized at the outset.

- There is no hierarchal order to the learning methods. Educational leaders can adopt or implement any learning method(s) in any order that suits their building's goals.

- There is much overlap of the learning methods. Strategies within each learning method cause these methods to have much in common. For example, an article in *Electronic Learning* announced interactive video, teacher presentation tools, electronic mail and a national bulletin board all under the umbrella of an Integrated Learning System (Hill 1993).

- These are learning methods for all learners and subject matters. These learning methods can be used with a wide range of talents and subjects. A learning method is not exclusively designed for a specific category of learner. Principals and planning teams should choose learning models to match the needs of particular students, subject material, level of expertise, or learning goals.

- Learning, particularly in the latter models, is an active process. Students are not recipients of instruction but active participants in choosing the depth and range of their own learning.

KEY QUESTION

What were the criteria for the selection of each of these Technology-Based Learning Methods?

Why were these technology-based learning methods chosen as examples? The selection criteria for each of these major methods of technology-based learning were 1) current use in education or industry; 2) use of technology to empower major learning strategies; and 3) all are within the domain of school change and emerging electronic learning technologies. The learning methods matrix on the following page (Figure 3—Learning Methods Matrix) provides an example of these major methods with a delineation of the center of control, major strategies within each method, and examples from business and industry. Learning centered methods implement the five competencies outlined by the *SCANS* (1991) report.

The TLM provides teachers with a useful conceptual tool to evaluate the role of technology in the educational process.

However, there are several other programs that provide educational change models that may occur simultaneously with the TLM and help to bring about overall restructuring or transformation of schools. Some of these are the six step plan of America 2000 (McREL 1990), overhaul of schooling infrastructure (Hodgkinson 1991), alternative methods for evaluation of student progress (Sizer 1992; Center for Children and Technology, Bank Street College 1990), and alternative school scheduling practices (Sizer 1992). English and Hill (1990) provided a useful outline of many differences between current educational practices and restructured schools.

Learning Methods Matrix

LEARNING METHOD	CENTER OF CONTROL	WORLD OF WORK EXAMPLE	STRATEGIES
Teacher-centered learning with technology	Teacher: The teacher directs the pace and sequence.	Training sessions, specific skill development	Multimedia presentation, videotape, distance instruction
Integrated learning systems	Machine: A computer network and its software direct the learning.	Teaching machines	Distributed ILS, lab centered ILS
Electronic collaborative learning	Teams/partners: The team negotiates goals, pacing, and sequence of learning.	Developmental teams, joint research efforts, learning teams	Local area networks, wide area networks, cooperative ventures
Hyperlearning	Learner: The learner is in charge of pace and sequence of learning.	Research, market analysis, engineering design	Hypertext development, hypermedia development, multimedia development, network searching
Electronic learning simulations	Machine and learner: Learning is in joint control.	Flight simulations, disaster control simulations, war games	Virtual reality electronic simulations

Figure 3

IRI/SkyLight Training and Publishing

KEY QUESTION

What are the critical elements of each TLM?

ELEMENTS OF THE LEARNING METHOD

To help the teachers navigate each technology-based learning method, there are nine elements which address specific issues. Each of these elements is identified by an ICON. Below are the nine elements and the corresponding ICON used in each learning method. They are in the order in which they appear within each learning method.

Element #1

The overview section of each method contains a one sentence concept of the methodology, the center of learning control, and a discussion on how this method can be used in the classroom.

Element #2

The payoffs section of each method lists advantages teachers can anticipate from adopting a technology-based learning method.

Element #3

The strategies section of each method outlines classroom strategies using emerging technologies that support a technology-based learning method.

Element #4

STAFF

The staff section sets out benefits and difficulties of the learning method for staff members. This section concludes with a discussion of what characteristics staff members using a technology-based learning method will exhibit.

Element #5

STUDENTS

The student section sets out benefits and difficulties of the learning method for students. This section concludes with a discussion of what characteristics students using a technology-based learning method will exhibit.

Element #6

FACILITIES

The facilities section of each method lists possible construction or remodeling concerns when adopting a technology-based learning method.

Element #7

BUDGET

The budget section of each method highlights financial considerations which must be examined when adopting a technology-based learning method.

Element #8

TIPS-TRICKS-TRAPS

This section provides useful techniques implementating a technology learning method along with some pitfalls to be avoided.

Element #9

EXAMPLES

As a final element in each Technology-Based Learning methods, a few examples of actual classroom use of technology have been included. These examples were selected from hundreds of possibilities. Often the examples chosen covered more than one Technology-Based Learning method. The illustrations were chosen to be exemplary, not comprehensive. Many more examples can be found in *Electronic Learning, The Computing Teacher,* and Betty Collis's *Computers, Curriculum and Whole-Class Instruction.*

SUMMARY

The core section of the Technology-Based Learning handbook is based on centers of learning. Five technology-based learning methods surrounding centers of learning and using emerging technology are examined: Teacher-Centered Learning with Technology (teacher), Integrated Learning Systems (machine), Electronic Collaborative Learning (learning team), Hyperlearning (individual learner), and Electronic Learning Simulations (machine and learner together). Each of these learning methods is clarified using nine elements: overview, strategies, payoffs, staff, students, facilities, budget, tips-trick-traps, and examples.

Recommended Readings for Chapter 4: Technology-Based Learning Methods

Bevilacqua, A. F. 1989. *Hypertext: Behind the hype.* (ERIC Document Reproduction Service No. ED 308 882).

Business Week. 1992. Reinventing America: Meeting the new challenges of a global economy. Special issue *Business Week No. 3191.*

Collis, B. 1988. *Computers, curriculum, and whole-class instruction.* Belmont, CA: Wadsworth.

English, F. W., and J. C. Hill. 1990. *Restructuring: The principal and curriculum change.* Reston, VA: National Association of Secondary School Principals.

Perelman, L. J. 1992. *School's out: Hyperlearning, the new technology, and the end of education.* New York: William Morrow.

U.S. Department of Labor. Secretary's Commission on Achieving Necessary Skills. 1991. *What work requires of schools: A SCANS report of America 2000.* Washington, D.C.: U. S. Government Printing Office.

Note

[1] It must be remembered that such a separation is an over simplification.

CHAPTER 5

Teacher-Centered Learning with Technology

*Teacher-centered learning is a **reform** methodology where classroom instructors maintain their traditional role but use emerging technologies as enhancements of instruction.*

> *A book is a machine to think with.*
>
> I. A. RICHARDS,
> PRINCIPLES OF LITERARY CRITICISM

KEY QUESTION

How do schools use technology to improve learning?

CONCEPT

Teacher-centered learning with technology uses technological enhancements to continue traditional instructional strategies.

CENTER OF LEARNING CONTROL

The teacher using emerging technology is the center of learning control.

DISCUSSION

In teacher-centered learning with technology, education is led by instructors using technology to enhance delivery of subject matter. Traditional strategies of lecture, dialogue, guided questions, and student evaluation continue unabated. However, new techniques of multimedia presentation, video display, distance teaching, and others are added dimensions to previous instructional strategies. In teacher-centered instruction, emerging technologies are tools of the instructional process. These technologies alter the basic pattern of instruction very little. Measurable student outcomes appear to be a strong feature of teacher-centered learning with technology.

Teacher-centered learning with technology, in the hands of skilled instructors, can be used in a variety of ways to enhance learning: drill and practice for review of basic skills, interaction with the class, individualization of lessons, motivation for learning, accessing different intelligences, instructional delivery across town or across the nation. Learning objectives are maintained by the classroom instructor. Teachers are provided new ways of presentation and reinforcement through technology.

Teacher-centered learning with technology has many of the same advantages as teacher-centered learning prior to the advent of electronic instructional technology. Among the advantages of teacher led instruction are

- Basic skill acquisition.

- Sequential introduction of new material.

- Measurable objectives and accomplishments.

Added to this list of advantages with teacher-centered instruction using technology are

- Renewed teacher enthusiasm.

- Increased student motivation.

- Better techniques for classroom demonstration.

- Increased accuracy in reporting results from student experiments.

- Greater visual portrayal of complex subjects.

- Increased sharing of scarce instructional resources through distance learning.

- Improved classroom lessons using multimedia: sound, graphics, video, animation.

There are several variations of teacher-centered learning with technology. They include

TEACHER PRESENTATION WITH TECHNOLOGY

Often in this strategy, multimedia presentation by teachers is analogous to lecture as a means of delivery. The teacher, at the front of the class, presents lessons using sound, graphics, animation, pictures, and video equipment controlled by a computer. In addition to a computer, equipment used in this strategy may include speakers, LCD panels, large monitors, video-tape machines, overhead projectors, and laser-disc machines (D'Ignazio 1990). Daiute (1992) makes an effective argument for using multimedia to teach basic reading and writing skills. This strategy views technology as a tool to enhance traditional educational programs, not a means to radically alter the educational process.

INDIVIDUAL STUDENT ASSIGNMENTS

Teachers direct students to complete homework assignments using electronic technologies. This may include computers and specific software programs for word processing (e.g. English), spread sheet (e.g., accounting), data-base (e.g. social studies), or computer-aided-drawing (e.g., industrial arts). Often these assignments need little sophisticated equipment. Math assignments can be completed using hand-held "talking" calculators. Writing assignments can be completed with "credit-card" size spell checkers.

MICRO-BASED LABORATORIES

Using appropriate scientific apparatus and software, computers measure, record, graph, and analyze a variety of physical properties such as temperature, light, pH, pressure, electrical, and mechanical properties (Morse 1991).

COMPUTER-ASSISTED INSTRUCTION (CAI)

In this strategy, a single computer can be used to provide or enhance instruction for students in a specific skill. It differs from an ILS in size of the management system, number of machines involved, and scope of material covered.

TEACHER-CENTERED LEARNING OVER DISTANCE

Many schools have found that instructional television delivered by broadcast, cable, or satellite has been an effective strategy to share scarce resources in several classrooms. Distance learning is the use of telecommunications equipment such as telephone, television fiber optics, cable broadcast, and satellites to send instructional programming to learners (Bruder 1991). Teacher-Centered Learning at a distance often uses television with students and teachers at different locations involved in two-way educational interaction. This strategy has been particularly valuable in isolated areas where classroom populations are small. The costs and talents of specialized teachers (e.g., foreign language, advanced science) can be shared among several school districts. Some states, Kentucky and Kansas for example, have invested heavily into distance television instruction.[1]

Many unresolved issues deter the effective use of a distance learning strategy. Among these issues are teacher certification, responsibility for the educational programming, and questions of teacher contracts and compensation. Isabelle Bruder (1989) outlined several concerns that must be addressed by teachers investigating distance learning strategies.

ONE-WAY PROGRAM DELIVERY

Many schools have opted to receive information in the classroom from one-way, non-interactive television. In this strategy, students are passive recipients of instruction, often current events or news programming. This information is delivered in much the same format as television at home. One leader in these efforts has been Chris Whittle's Channel 1. It is estimated that one-third of the America's teenagers view current events programming provided at no charge to each school by Whittle Communications. (Tienne 1993). Other popular sources of educational television programming have been National Public Broadcasting and National Geographic.

Teachers find the ability to present complex material with electronic enhancements exhilarating. They can visually present difficult concepts. Teachers, by using art and authoring packages, can make attractive visuals. Events difficult to observe because of time, distance, danger, or rarity can be realistically recreated. Apple Corporation describes teacher presentation stations as one of the main delivery tools for multimedia (Apple Corp. 1990).

weakness.

However, unless teachers have adequate training using these materials, the process can be very frustrating and confusing. Teacher centered instruction with technology is highly dependent upon teachers' attitude towards this means of instructing children. Teachers must be comfortable with electronic devices they are given to enhance instruction. Developing instructional competence and confidence with emerging technological equipment is one of the crucial needs of integrating technology in their schools. Staff development for teachers is an often overlooked or underfunded aspect of technology integration in schools. In fulfilling their leadership role, administrators seek, support, and cultivate educators who are able to

- Evaluate and use software in different educational settings.

- Describe the purposes and major features of application software.

- Identify sources for computer education materials in all subject areas.

- Relate learning theory and principles of child development to the creation of a computer learning environment.

- Discuss major issues in computer education.

- Apply their knowledge of curriculum development to develop supplemental materials to use with computer software.

- Develop a few simple programs or products using technology.

- Interpret research findings, theory, and literature in the field.

- Discuss characteristic strengths and weaknesses of different programming languages (Adams & Hamm 1987).[2]

What would staff members' use of teacher-centered learning technology method look like?

- Teachers taking risks in lesson preparation with technology.

- Teachers leading attractive, exciting activities with technology.

- Teachers addressing a variety of student needs and learning styles with technology.

- Teachers at different levels of multimedia instructional expertise: authoring, using, and experimenting.

Depending upon the emerging technology used by the instructor, students benefit from many different instructional elements. Often these demonstration technologies allow material to be placed in a visual framework. Teacher demonstrations of mathematical solutions or scientific experiments are examples of using a computer and projection device. Video technology allows students to see contemporary versions of famous stories performed by classical actors. Multimedia technologies allow for comparative versions of the same learning material. Distance learning technologies allow students to follow instruction in one location led by an instructor in another. This technology allows schools separated by distance to share the benefits of teacher specialization and expertise.

Students benefit from technology by having time consuming, repetitive examples presented numerous ways using interesting graphics and other multi-sensory techniques. Examples of this strategy are seen in the emphasis on calculators and graphing calculators in the new math standards (Bruder, Buchsbaum, Hill, & Orlando 1992). Demonstrations also allow simulated practice with situations which are too dangerous or rare to practice in real life.

What should principals look for when observing students using teacher-centered learning technology methods?

- Students show increased enthusiasm for classroom lessons.

- Students demonstrate a deeper understanding of complex material.

- Students demonstrate a faster comprehension of complex material.

- Students demonstrate a greater connection between classroom learning and real world examples.

- Students demonstrate learning that addresses their unique intelligence.

- Students enrolled in classes offered and taught by instructors in different locations.

FACILITIES

Teacher-centered instruction using emerging technology may take little facility revision. Most electronic instruction can proceed with no modification to traditional classrooms. Lighting, electrical power, and projection areas are basic considerations. These need to be addressed in construction or remodeling projects. Many classrooms are sufficient with little modification.

Much of the emerging technology equipment used in teacher-centered mode of instruction can be placed on carts and moved around school buildings that meet guidelines for handicapped accessibility. Equipment can be stored in central locations and checked out to teachers as needed. If connection to a network is needed, additional wiring will be required.

However, if distance learning via television is chosen as a strategy, facility requirements can be extensive. The Minnesota Department of Education found planning and construction for television demonstration stations cost between $131,400 and $1,082,805. Their annualized operating costs averaged $56,435. (Morehouse, Hoaglund & Schmidt 1987). Conversely, thousands of dollars of video equipment has been placed in classrooms around the nation at no cost to school districts by Whittle Communications (Rist 1991).

BUDGET

Budgeting for teacher instructional centers is extremely flexible. Expenditures are tailored to subject matter. Some subjects may require a great deal of expense for software; others may not.

Deborah Branscum (1992) suggested five strategies to save money when purchasing technology hardware and software.

SHAREWARE-FREEWARE

User groups and others belonging to on-line systems find surprisingly good software available over modems or for purchase through user groups at reasonable prices.

LOW-COST COMMERCIAL SOFTWARE

Unless there is a specific need for powerful drawing, spreadsheet or word processing programs, many low cost, reasonably featured packages, are available in the $50.00–$200.00 range.

INTEGRATED PACKAGES

While integrated packages usually cost more than low-end, stand alone software programs, they offer good value for the money. Most integrated packages include word processing, data base, spreadsheet, and draw modules.

USED HARDWARE

Good used equipment can be purchased through local classified ads, computer brokers, or direct-mail companies. However, care and technical expertise may be required to insure that such equipment is in good condition and meets the software requirements for memory and processing speed.

PENNY-PINCHERS

Many companies offer program upgrades at reasonable prices. There are many direct mail catalogs that offer significant savings in price.

Deborah Branscum addressed her money saving techniques toward the purchase of computer equipment. Teachers working on a "tight budget" should not over look local electronic stores for many of their technology purchases.[3]

Another tactic to pursue is leasing equipment. This tactic may provide a way to acquire significant quantities of expensive equipment and at the same time avoid having the school saddled with expensive equipment that rapidly becomes obsolete. Apple and IBM both provide leasing or lease purchase options for schools.

TIPS-TRICKS-TRAPS

TIPS

TIP #1 If technology resources are going to be shared by teachers from room to room, make sure the cart they are to be carried on is sturdy, has large wheels for rolling over obstructions, and is equipped to "plug and play." The equipment must only need one plug-in and one switch to turn everything on. Also, be sure the cart is checked out as a unit. Individual devices and cables must remain with the cart and not be "scavenged" for other uses. Insure that an individual is assigned responsibility for maintaining and scheduling the equipment.

TIP #2

"Grantsmanship" is an effective strategy for getting resources for the classroom. Often school districts, to encourage innovative practices in the classroom, have grant programs. Before authorizing these grants, check to make sure these grants match the curriculum goals of the school.

TIP #3

Principals can encourage teachers to form partnerships with local businesses to provide technology learning experiences for students. Some corporations provide mini-grants.

TIP #4

Some teachers are reluctant to use technology in their classrooms because technology means more work for them. To win over these reluctant users, ways in which technology can ease the workload of classroom teachers must be provided. Two ways to do this may be to provide computers to each teacher and electronic mail for communication.

TIP #5

Teachers must model technology use for their students. Students must see the teachers using emerging technologies for both instruction and management. Teachers who "preach" technology but do not "practice" technology send conflicting messages to students. Staff development for teachers is absolutely essential. This staff development must be at two levels: skills level and conceptual level. There are sources specific to staff development such as Bailey and Lumley (1994).

TIP #6

Many strategies and tactics for acquiring funds to initiate and institute technology-based learning methods can be gleaned from the work of others. David Bauer (1993) has published a series of monographs that outline effective ways of developing the financial resources necessary to institutionalize a technology-based learning method.

TRICKS

TRICK #1

Students using technology for School Board demonstrations, "Parent's Night," or community programs are effective ways of building support for the school technology program. Insure these audiences understand how this technology is used every day in the business world and how the students are gaining skills they will use after they complete their formal education.

TRICK #2
Finding ways to use equipment as it becomes outdated is on-going strategy to expand the use of technology in schools. Much of this equipment can start students on new ways of communication using multimedia projects. Fred D'Ignazio (1989a, 1989b, 1990e, 1991a) designed programs around "scavenged" equipment for multimedia.

TRICK #3
Planned abandonment is a necessary part of integrating technology into the regular classroom. Schools must plan for abandoning outdated instructional practices and equipment. Tradition or community standards often hinder efforts to eliminate some outdated programs and practices. Abandonment of tried and traditional practices is often controversial. For example, *What is the role of the "County Spelling Bee" in a curriculum full of spell checkers?*

TRAPS

TRAP #1
Technology equipment used only for remediation or reward is often unconnected to the curriculum. This technology does not become part of the curriculum, but serves as an "add on" to the regular program. Parents who see kids "playing games" may be observing technology unconnected to the curriculum. Teachers must insure that technologies are used to support curricular purposes.

TRAP #2
Teachers are often given or request technology equipment for their classroom with little or no training in its effective instructional use. For effective use of technology in classrooms, teachers must have the skills to run the equipment, an understanding of how the equipment enhances student learning, and the opportunity to practice both. These technology skills can materialize only through effective, on-going, technology staff development activities.

EXAMPLES

HANDS ON MATH AND SCIENCE

In an Alabama school science class, a variety of sensors and probes are connected to Macintosh computers. This effectively changes the computer into an oscilloscope, temperature probe, pressure sensor, or light meter. Students use this equipment to make science come alive through hands-on activities. They take control of physics and chemistry experiments and, given the greater accuracy of the computer sensors, the students are able to develop projects that come closer to theoretical values (McCarthy 1992).

WRITING TO LEARN

A class of low achieving students was loaned a roomful of IBM *PC Jrs.* to help these students learn how to write effectively. Suddenly, the classroom was changed from a room of low achievers to one of high achieving students writing longer sentences and sentences with purpose. The instructor felt there was a major shift in student attitudes about writing. Some of the previously low achieving students signed up to take the Advanced Placement class in English (Hill 1992c).

BEYOND DRILL AND PRACTICE IN A ONE-COMPUTER CLASSROOM

Even with minimal equipment, enthusiastic instructors develop effective learning activities that accomplish goals established by the teacher. One example was a second grade classroom with only one computer. An enthusiastic teacher was able to have students write letters of at least five sentences. By rotating the use of the computer it took twenty-two students six days to write their letters. For the next assignment, this teacher used the one computer to write a cooperative geography report. The first software package the students used was *Magic Slate*. They soon advanced to *Children's Writing and Publishing Center*. "When you do drill and practice at the computer, the computer is in charge of the learning. When you word process, the person at the keyboard is truly the master of his or her own learning."(Weisberg 1992).

GAINING FLUENCY

The staff of a classroom of special needs students wanted to help their class access a modern language curriculum. They started by using a Canon *Ion* still video camera. After returning to school from a field trip to a local French grocery store, the pictures were viewed as a vehicle for discussing the experience. One of the instructors used a software package to create an on-screen supermarket. These special need students stocked the shelves using the appropriate foreign language labels (Hughes 1992).

BLACKBOARD-DISK JOCKEYS

With five computers and one CD-ROM, a kindergarten teacher used technology to study language arts and science. The instructor was particularly pleased that the students were able to make their own choices as they navigated through the CD-ROM. The CD-ROM addressed many learning styles: visual, auditory, and tactile (Hill 1993a).

THE STUDENT MAESTRO

At a variety of schools, from inner-city to rural, music educators are using technology to change student perceptions about music. Included in the technologies being used to bring about this change have been MTV, CD-ROMS, and keyboards. Using Yamaha's *Music in Education* series, students have listened, played, and learned various aspects of music composition. In one school an innovative teacher asked students to choose a song from their favorite musical group. Using *HyperCard* stacks and Voyager's *CD Audio Toolkit,* students annotated the composition with text and graphics (Solomon 1993).

LIGHTS, ACTION, MATH

Three new programs were used to lead instruction for the integration of the National Council of Teachers of Mathematics's math standards. The first of the three programs was *Fundamental Math.* This was a series of video tapes containing 30 specific math concepts. The second was Tom Snyder's *The Graph Club,* which was an integrated graphing tool package, a manipulative software environment, and a comprehensive curriculum guide. The third was *Hands-On Math,* which was a computer simulation of 17 lessons using math manipulatives such as rods, counters, and number balance (Lindroth 1994).

THE HIGH SCHOOL OFFICE

The office practice classroom of the future looked just like the office of modern corporation. It was furnished with up-to-date equipment including computers, FAX, copy machines, and telephones. Students were involved in activities that might be associated with corporate offices and workplaces. There was a general feeling of purposeful activity and attention to business. The difference was the "office" was in a school; and students were using technology to master modern business skills (Apple Computer Inc. 1991).

VIDEO NETWORK TO CONNECT STUDENTS IN SEVEN SCHOOLS

Space-age technology has given students in small rural communities more class choices and opportunities for learning. Seven schools in a rural area joined together to create a fiber optic network that allowed students to interact with students in distant classrooms. Additionally, students enrolled in courses that small schools could not afford to provide. Each school was able to capitalize on the strengths of their teaching staff (Bittinger 1991).

TECHNOLOGY IN SPECIAL EDUCATION

In a Michigan High School students with special needs visited a room with three computers. The purpose for this visitation was to help these students catch up with assignments established in traditional classrooms. Some of the students had learning disabilities, some had emotional impairments, and others had attention deficit disorders. All, however, were behind in traditional course work. The use of the three computers in this classroom allowed the students to catch up with their assignments because they wrote faster and the technology maintained their interest (Holzberg 1994).

Recommended Readings for Chapter 5: Teacher-Centered Learning with Technology

Bailey, G. D., and D. Lumley. 1993. *Technology staff development programs: A leadership sourcebook for administrators*. New York: Scholastic.

Bauer, D. G. 1993. *The principal's guide to grant success*. New York: Scholastic.

Bruder, I., H. Buchsbaum, M. Hill, and L. C. Orland. 1992. School reform: Why you need technology to get there. *Electronic Learning 11(8)*: 22–28.

Buerry, L., K. Haslan, and N. Legters. 1990. Images of potential: From vision to reality. Special Reprint from *Business Week No. 3191:* 50–53.

Dede, C. 1987. Empowering environments, hypermedia and microworlds. *The Computing Teacher 15(3)*: 20–24.

D'Ignazio, F. 1989. Getting started with multimedia: 16 classroom strategies. *The Computing Teacher 16(3)*: 17–19.

Lumley, D., and G. D. Bailey. 1993. *Planning for technology: A guidebook for school administrators*. New York: Scholastic.

Whisler, J. S. 1988. Distance learning technologies: An aid to restructuring schools? In Mid-Continent Regional Educational Laboratory, *Noteworthy*, Washington, DC: U. S. Government Printing Office, 28–41.

Notes

[1] See Transparency TCL-1 for an example of a distance learning network in Southwest Kansas.

[2] The International Society for Technology in Education (ISTE) submitted to the National Council of Accreditation Education (NCATE) its recommendations for a set of national accreditation standards for education technology. These make a suitable "starting point" for principals seeking to determine the qualities needed by their computer using instructional staff members.

[3] See Transparency TCL-2 for a graphical review of money saving techniques.

CHAPTER 6

Integrated Learning System

Integrated Learning System (ILS) is a restructuring methodology where computer networks and management systems provide a substantial portion of basic skills instruction.

> *The real problem is not whether machines think, but whether men [sic] do.*
> B. F. Skinner

KEY QUESTION

How can schools using technology help students in reading, writing, and math?

CONCEPT

Students using an Integrated Learning System (ILS) accomplish specific learning outcomes using computer technologies, systematic monitoring, and incremental, behavioral computer-driven teaching.

CENTER OF LEARNING CONTROL

The computer network and its administrative software controls the learning process.

DISCUSSION

Integrated Learning Systems are perhaps the largest single comprehensive use of the emerging technologies in the United States. A recent estimate placed the number of schools which own an ILS at 7,947 (*Electronic Learning* 1992a). Currently, the United States invests nearly half a billion dollars annually in ILS (Butzin 1992).

An ILS consists of networked hardware that uses complex management systems to provide individualized basic skills instruction (*Electronic Learning,* 1992). The traditional delivery of instruction through the use of an ILS is a networked facility sharing software between a large number of computers and a file server. The file server directs and monitors the flow of information to and from the other computers (Lumley & Bailey 1990). Integrated Learning Systems dovetail with outcome-based methods. They provide teachers with opportunities for reteaching and establishing mastery levels (Mageau 1992). Often, an ILS has been positioned more to provide supplemental and remedial instruction than mainstream instruction.

ILS software connects computer devices to accomplish the following instructional tasks:

- Assessment and diagnosis of student skills.

- Delivery of instruction.

- Continuous monitoring of student performance with automatic instructional adjustment.

- Generation of student and class performance data. (Maddux & Willis 1992).

PAYOFFS

Achievement outcomes for students using an ILS have been a source of controversy. ILSs are in large measure established to produce and document measurable gains in basic skills. A number of critics have attacked ILSs, noting they failed to support higher order thinking skills (Sherry 1990; Trotter 1990). Becker (1992) challenged ILSs when they are used as the sole component of effective instruction. Still some specific benefits have been documented by student outcomes research.

- Student excitement at working on computers (Trotter 1990; Sherry 1990b).

- Parents and administrators appreciated printed reports on student's progress (Trotter 1990).

- Individualized instruction matched to the curriculum (Trotter 1990; Sherry 1990b).

- Color graphics (Trotter 1990).

STRATEGIES

Currently there are two instructional strategies using an ILS: laboratory placements and distributed placement.

LABORATORY PLACEMENT

The first, and more common, placement of an ILS is in a laboratory. Students are sent or escorted to work in the ILS lab. The labs are usually supervised by monitors familiar with the equipment and software, but lacking formal teacher training. Teachers, through

the management system, establish lessons, mastery levels, and reporting schedules. They often do not accompany their students to the lab to supervise their work. This delivery strategy focuses on ILS as a supplement to mainstream classroom instruction. There is a high correlation with traditional textbooks in an ILS lab placement.

DISTRIBUTED PLACEMENT

In the second delivery model, ILS networks are distributed throughout the building in individual classrooms. Teachers manage the same functions as with a lab-oriented ILS, but with small groups of students at workstations in the classroom. Distributed ILS networks become an integral part of classroom instruction in this model, not a supplemental or "pull out" remedial program. Teachers personally supervise student progress. Instructors maintain a subjective grasp on student learning patterns.

Staff considerations for an ILS methodology are dependent on the type of placement established for the equipment. If a laboratory placement for an ILS program is chosen, a lab supervisor needs to be hired and trained. The lab supervisors do not need to be fully certified teachers. The lab supervisors need familiarity with the administrative program of the ILS. The lab supervisors need an understanding of the art of teaching to insure the learning goals of teachers are being addressed by the programming received through an ILS.

If a distributed ILS is chosen, all teachers involved with the ILS need training in the administrative program. The teachers must be able to insure assignments and goals established for students are met. Classroom instructors must also be able to generate meaningful reports on a timely basis.

In some ways, hiring a lab monitor to address the teachers' needs through an ILS is easier than training all teachers in managing the intricacies of an ILS management system. The lab monitor and classroom teacher must be able to communicate. Although a lab supervisior is more expensive and may be less effective, greater confidence for successful supervision of the ILS comes from knowing it is one person's sole responsibility. The cheaper alternative, distributed networks, relies on classroom teachers and requires high levels of training, motivation, and supervision.

What would staff members' use of Integrated Learning Systems look like?

- Classroom curriculum goals incorporated into ILS instruction.

- Use of reporting and management capabilities of the ILS.

- Regular monitoring of student progress.

- Regular use of the ILS system to match student achievement to curriculum objectives.

- Effective communication between a lab monitor and instructional staff.

STUDENTS

Specific learning goals are established in incremental, behavioral steps. Students meet these goals through one of two ILS placements: a lab placement or distributed placement. In the former students leave their regular classroom for the ILS lab where they receive instruction via the equipment. In the latter, students remain in their regular classroom receiving programmed instruction under the tutelage of the regular classroom teacher. Students need little training to use an ILS.

What would students' use of Integrated Learning Systems look like?

- Self-paced learning.

- Specific, documented achievement outcomes.

- ILS as an integral part of classroom instruction.

- Subject mastery for all students at different times.

FACILITIES

A lab arrangement for an ILS requires a specialized room sufficiently large to hold 20–25 students, an instructor's station, the associated server, and printers to accompany ILS programs. Several factors must be addressed in the design of the ILS lab:[1]

- Lighting

- Furniture

- Wiring

- Security

- Storage for software, paper, and supplies

- Telephone connection for modem and technical communications with vendor.

SPECIALIZED MATERIALS FOR ILS INCLUDE

- Many computers.

- Dedicated server.

- Mass storage devices.

- Printers.

- Network wiring and devices.

- Specialized administrative software.

- Specialized subject software.

BUDGET

Depending on the courseware purchased with the installation, one recent estimate established the cost of a 25-station student ILS lab at $50,000–$125,000 (Sherry 1992b). Additional costs include:

- Software licensing, update or support fees ($100–$45,000 yearly).

- Staff training if not included in basic vendor's pricing.

- Electrical wiring charges.

- Developing available space for an ILS lab. (Sherry 1992b).

A different analysis set the cost of an ILS lab at $3,000 per work station and $50–$750 per station for software enhancements, updates and upgrades (Finkel 1992).

Risks are proportional to anticipated expenses. When shopping for expensive integrated learning systems, many factors should be considered before investing in such a major capital expenditure.

- Define the need.

- Audit the present curriculum.

- Consider alternatives.

- Involve all significant stakeholders: administrators, teachers, students, and parents.

- Insure a strong correlation between ILS courseware and curriculum.

- Plan for adequate money and personnel resources to support the ILS system.

- Look for hidden costs.

- Start with a pilot project.

- Avoid purchasing "vaporware." (Untried software in development to be released in the future).

- Look to the financial health and stability of the selected vendor.

- Make sure the system includes productive tools such as a good word processing program.

- Give ample training to teachers who are to use the ILS.
  (Trotter 1990).

- Ensure the ILS lab meets acceptable standards for comfort, safety, and utility.

- Determine if an ILS lab or distributed ILS network suits the building's needs.

TIPS-TRICKS-TRAPS

TIPS

TIP #1

A special edition of *Electronic Learning* (1992a) listed several tips involving school administration which would help out for the effective integration of an ILS:

- Principals must be the ILS leader by modeling and creating excitement for the ILS with their teachers.

- Principals must help teachers overcome reluctance based on "technophobia."

- Principals must hold regular in-service workshops for teachers to demonstrate the features of an ILS.

- Principals should hire competent ILS managers who have instructional backgrounds.

- Principals should insure the reports generated by an ILS are used to communicate with parents and modify educational programming.

- Principals should provide correlational charts for the ILS and the instructional curriculum.

TIP #2   Investigate carefully the financial background of the ILS corporation being considered. Schools do not want to make a major purchase of an ILS system with a firm that is about to go out of business.

TIP #3   Order more printers. They will be used.

TRICKS

TRICK #1   Enthusiasm can be built and perhaps generate funds for an ILS by providing adult literacy programs with the system during non-traditional school hours.

TRICK #2   Several ILS and software developers are producing third-party programs that run with an ILS management system. This gives teachers expanded options when choosing software packages.

TRAPS

TRAP #1   Management systems can be extremely difficult to use. Having little support from the vendor can bring a well-planned ILS to a halt. Management system support should be thoroughly investigated and compared before purchase.

Annual licensing or update fees for ILS software can be expensive. Investigate and plan for these costs as an ongoing expense.

 An ILS purchased exclusively with Title I or disadvantaged monies may have to be dedicated solely to serving a specific class of students.

EXAMPLES

WRITING TO READ

In a large scale California demonstration project to evaluate the *Writing to Read* program, (IBM Corporation) four networked computers were used in kindergarten and first grade classrooms. Networking the computers freed students from having to work with disks and allowed them to log on independently throughout the school day. Teachers developed daily lesson units tailored to specific needs of students. Networked software was made available to support classroom goals. Several instruments for evaluation were used. These included classroom observations, pre- and post-test scores from reading attitude surveys, year-long portfolios, interviews, and questionnaires. The major conclusions of this study were that students had more positive attitudes towards reading and writing and greater success than those in traditional classrooms (Anderson-Inman 1994).

INTEGRATING AN ILS:
TWO TEACHING MODELS THAT WORK

In one model for using an Integrated Learning System the computers were centralized in one location. Students left the regular classroom to work in an ILS lab. This school was committed to achieving an outcomes-based curriculum. The teachers first endorsed the curriculum and later bought into using an ILS as a means of providing this curriculum.

A second model for an ILS distributed the equipment throughout the classrooms. Teachers retained greater control over the ILS and the student's learning. During the early phases of this distribution, teachers used the ILS as another classroom resource, not the central part of the curriculum. It was not until later that instructional delivery, through the ILS, became central to the classroom educational program (Mageau 1992).

PROJECT CHILD

By combining altered instruction scheduling with an ILS, the Florida based Project CHILD created a new program for integrating instructional technology with regular classroom teaching. Three classrooms formed a CHILD cluster. Each teacher became a content specialist in addition to working with one class. Each of the classrooms was organized with ILS learning stations appropriate for the teacher's content specialty. The software provided with the program encouraged higher-order thinking and applied learning skills. An essential part of this program was daily use of the technology. Project CHILD has been validated by the Program Effectivnesss Panel of the U.S. Department of Education's National Diffusion Network (Butzin 1992).

ILS: ITS NEW ROLE IN SCHOOLS

A California school with nearly 70% of its students from a minority population and nearly 60% of the students living below the poverty line posted impressive academic achievements. The district administration attributed their high rate of success to a district-wide commitment to an Integrated Learning System. Installed in every K–1 classroom in this district was an IBM *Writing to Read* lab. Each 2–6 grade classroom had three IBM PS/2 Model 25 computers connected to a distributed network. The file servers carried Wasatch Educational System software for language arts, math, and science. Also included in the network software were learning tools for students, which included a word processor, glossary, notebook calculator, graphing program, and electronic mail. This equipment and software were all purchased with state and local monies and IBM grants. No Chapter 1 funds were used (Mageau 1990).

THE SATURN SCHOOL

The Saturn School was established to blend the best methods of existing schools with the powerful emerging technologies. Access to technology played a key role for teachers and students in establishing an individualized learning environment. Teachers focused on individual students by using Integrated Learning Systems as well as stand-alone software. Both Josten's and Computer Curriculum Corporation ILS were in place. The Josten's system presented information using color graphics and video. The Computer Curriculum Corporation system was more straightforward and responsive to learner's performance.

Recommended Readings for Chapter 6: Integrated Learning Systems

Bailey, G. D., ed. 1992. *Computer-based integrated learning systems*. Englewood Cliffs, NJ: Educational Technology Publications.

Electronic Learning. 1991. Integrated learning systems: How to buy an ILS. *Electronic Learning*. Special supplement. Winter: 6–12.

Finkel, L. 1992. Are ILS worth the $$? *Electronic Learning 12(1)*: 18.

Sherry, M. 1990. Implementing an integrated instructional system. *Phi Delta Kappan 72(2)*: 118–20.

White, M. A. 1989. Educators must ask themselves some important questions. *Electronic Learning 9(1)*: 6–7.

———. 1992. Are ILSs good education? *Educational Technology 32(9)*: 49–50.

Note

[1] See Transparency ILS-1 for a facilities checklist when considering the purchase of an ILS.

CHAPTER 7

Electronic Collaborative Learning

Electronic collaborative learning is a
transformational *methodology where*
learners using networking strategies work
together as teams on projects over time
and distance.

> *The next breakthrough won't be in the individual interface but in the team interface.*
>
> JOHN SEELY BROWN

KEY QUESTION:

How can technology help schools develop student learning teams?

CONCEPT

Using electronic network and display technologies, learners work together to create, access, discover, and share information in collaborative efforts.

CENTER OF LEARNING CONTROL

In electronic collaborative learning, the learning team is the center of learning control.

DISCUSSION

Principals should grasp that there are two halves with overlapping strategies in electronic collaborative learning: 1) cooperative learning and 2) collaborative learning.

Johnson & Johnson (1991) and Slavin (1983) outlined the essential features of cooperative learning. The essential feature of their work was the development of cooperative learning learning teams as a strategy for enhancing educational opportunities for children. Johnson and Johnson and Slavin developed and tested models for improving student performance in the classroom by developing learning teams.

Educational network collaboration is a more recent addition to instructional methods. Even though the two terms have separate meanings, opportunities for developing electronic networking have created conditions which allow cooperation and collaboration in school settings. The design of electronic collaborative learning is to make "the boundaries between classrooms and class periods more permeable" (Newman 1992, 312). Electronic collaboration is designed to allow students to work together on learning projects between schools and at different times.

In the reality of educational practice, boundaries have been established that are both physical (walls and distance) and timely (class periods and school days). These boundaries have limited opportunities for cooperative learning in single classrooms and class periods. Electronic collaborative learning allows students to overcome these boundaries and work as teams over time and distance. They can work cooperatively or collaboratively. The teacher is a facilitator and collaborator in the learning process.

"Cooperative learning is a structured process built on the belief that we learn better when we learn together" (Bruder 1992, 18). Cooperation implies agreement between individuals towards a common learning goal. Groups succeed or fail, regardless of individual success or failure. Cooperative learning contains a concept of group evaluation to collectively earn rewards based upon the group's effort (Slavin 1983). Cooperative learning implies a level of behaviorism. There is a lesson for the group to learn. The SCANS report identified the ability to cooperatively work together as one of the crucial skills for the world of work in the year 2000 (U. S. Department Labor 1991).

Collaboration denotes a different aspect from cooperative learning. Collaboration is an act of shared creation or shared discovery (Schrage 1990). Collaboration does not imply "getting along." In fact, some notable artistic collaborators had furious arguments (Schrage 1990). However it does imply the development of previously undiscovered knowledge as different from cooperatively learning that which was already known.

Clearly, cooperation and collaboration are significant learning methods. Both cooperation and collaboration maintain a strong emphasis on shared talents and group efforts toward learning common outcomes. Electronic networks support and expand these learning opportunities. Electronic networks add power to cooperative and collaborative learning, transforming them into new and unique learning methods. These electronic networks and the skills to work together have become critical features of schooling in the Information-Age.

A significant benefit of networking strategies within cooperative or collaborative learning environments is the opportunity for students to interact over both time and distance. Students no longer have to be face-to-face to work collaboratively or cooperatively. They can be in different buildings, towns, or countries and meet at different times.

PAYOFFS

Johnson and Johnson (1991) and Slavin (1983) noted positive outcomes for cooperative learning in both the cognitive and affective domains. These positive outcomes included significant cognitive achievement in problem solving and group production. In the affective domain, attitudes toward instructional activities, self-esteem, and intergroup relations improved. Electronic technologies add dimension to these cooperative benefits by allowing cooperative learning over time and space. When working together on a computer, Johnson and Johnson (1985) listed that students could

- Observe and imitate each other's use of the computer.

- Observe, imitate, and build upon each other's strategies, thereby increasing mastery.

- Experience the encouragement, support, warmth, and approval or classmates.

- Have peers evaluate, diagnose, correct, and give feedback on understanding.

- Have greater exposure to diverse ideas and procedures.

- Develop more critical thinking and more creative responses.

Adding to Johnson and Johnson's outcomes from cooperative learning, Schrage (1990) listed benefits of technology through enhanced media that integrated the intellectual virtues of print, the appeal of television, and the information handling power of computers. To Schrage, the media may be the message, but collaboration redefined the meaning of both media and message.

STRATEGIES

There are several strategies for electronic collaborative and cooperative learning. The essential non-electronic features of these have been outlined by Slavin (1983) and Johnson and Johnson (1991).

Recognizing Johnson and Johnson's efforts, how can technology enhance student cooperative learning? Four strategies seem most appropriate for maximizing the benefits of electronic cooperative or collaborative learning over time and space: same time–same place, same time–different place, different time–same place, and different time–different place (Johnson 1991).

SAME TIME–SAME PLACE

Students in the same classroom work together with the equipment in discovering or creating course materials. Face-to-face electronic collaborative learning uses technology to develop solutions to group problems. Students can employ shared display devices (monitors and LCD panels) or share input devices (keyboards and electronic pointers).

SAME TIME–DIFFERENT PLACE

In this strategy learners work at different places connected by electronic networks. These learners may be across the nation, across town, or across the hall. They may be connected by a phone line, microwave tower, or satellite. All students meet at the same time to develop products or understandings but at different places. Wide area networks

(WAN) may be employed to work with students across the nation. Local area networks (LAN) can be used for students to experience collaboration with students in the next classroom.

DIFFERENT TIME–SAME PLACE

In this strategy learners work together on the same project, on the same work stations, but at different times to meet the needs of their individual life styles. Work stations or terminals have the capability to store team members' work for later reference by other members of the team. A LAN allows students to store electronic documents on a network server for other students to work on at a later time. Electronic mail (E-mail) is a common communication technology of this strategy.

DIFFERENT TIME–DIFFERENT PLACE

In this strategy, information is developed and forwarded for electronic collaborative learning to other locales to be worked on later. This strategy appears to be a useful technique when collaboratively learning over distance and through several time zones. These devices are connected electronically and have the ability to store team members' progress.

TIME–SHIFTING PLACE–SHIFTING COLLABORATION

A rapidly emerging strategy, not seen by Johnson, seems to be a fluid collaboration between students, experts, faculty, and the public. The rapid growth of the Internet in all its forms—Web browsers, electronic mail, LISTSERVs, new groups—has created an electronic environment where groups can meet to share and grow in knowledge and understanding. Students may "lurk on the net" with little participation, join and quit groups at will, or communicate with a wide range of individuals. They are no longer limited by time, place, or team members. Learning teams come and go as interest grows and declines. The technologies of the Internet, its easy access, and its friendly environment present learning opportunities just recently available to students. Teachers who fail to incorporate this new technology as part of their learning collaboration methodology risk missing an opportunity to expand the horizons of student learning out of the bounds established by traditional instruction.

Staff electronic collaboration is an important benefit to electronic collaboration for students. Teacher isolation has been identified as one factor retarding the development of common instructional goals (Goodlad 1984). Teachers, as well as students, can use electronic mail and other similar technologies to overcome the "isolation factor" of educational programs. Teachers electronically connected over networks develop and share with colleagues across the hall or across town. These teachers find electronic networks are invaluable resources for improving instructional programming. Teachers can professionally communicate with each other more effectively if they have networking capabilities in their classrooms (McREL 1992). Added to the potential for teacher collaboration with colleagues throughout the building is the potential for teachers to collaborate with others around the world. Sharing ideas, developing curriculum, and writing lesson plans are no longer isolated activities. Teachers can now share with other teachers via networks from their desks. Administrative burdens—attendance, grade reporting, accounting—can be lightened through electronic building or district networks.

To employ electronic collaborative and cooperative learning strategies, teachers need a firm grasp of cooperative and collaborative learning without technology. They can weld electronic technology to these models to improve and expand opportunities for student collaboration.

Networking computers is a complex series of technological skills that must be mastered by teachers to effectively communicate. These skills appear to be

1. Basic computer operation.

2. Shared computer operation over a LAN with a dedicated server.

3. Electronic mail.

4. MODEM or other computer communication device.

Grunwald (1991) outlined an eight-step plan to provide for instructional networking in the classroom.

1. Provide telephone lines.

2. Provide hardware.

3. Provide software.

4. Consider standardizing software.

5. Select and budget for services.

6. Provide initial training.

7. Encourage use.

8. Provide ongoing training.

What would teachers' use of electronic collaborative learning technology methods look like?

- Ability of teachers to manage cooperative learning activities.

- Collaboration of teachers over time and distance.

- Sharing of scarce data management resources.

- Aid in creating a common school culture through staff communication.

- Encouraging students to develop collaborative and cooperative skills electronically.

- A movement away from whole-class instruction toward more collaborative work in small groups (Newman 1992).

Given sufficient training and equipment, electronic collaborative learning provides an effective learning method for a wide range of students. Special emphasis has been placed on these methods for children with exceptionalities. With growing diversity in the classroom, electronic network technologies hold extra promise for incorporating exceptional children into the mainstream classroom (Male 1986). The very uniqueness of these students adds to the value of the electronic cooperative and collaborative projects. Linda Roberts, a senior associate of the U. S. Congress, Office of Technology and Assessment, expressed a firm conviction that telecommunications greatly expanded both the quality and quantity of information resources available in the classroom (Leslie 1993).

Classroom network activities need to be well structured. Specific rules for collaboration and discussion must be clearly spelled out and enforced. Controls must be set to insure all students have opportunities to express themselves, yet not dominate equipment or the communication lines. Group and individual assessment plans must be clearly spelled out.

In order to insure student success with network use, teachers, administrators, students, and school board members must join to draft policies and procedures for network use which fit community standards. Networking, whether locally or internationally, possesses some hazards which should be addressed early in the implementation phase of this learning methodology. Failing to do this in the early stages and failing to insure that these standards are clearly communicated to all participants leads to reactions which would have the effect of denying student access to electronic collaborative learning.

What would students' use of electronic collaborative learning technology methods look like?

- Student collaboration over time and distance.

- Increased ability of students to access and analyze data.

- Student ability to use electronic technology to work together to achieve common goals.

- Increased student acceptance of other students from different backgrounds and cultures.

FACILITIES

Facility planning for electronic collaborative or cooperative learning stations has several aspects depending upon the strategy desired.

CLASSROOM COLLABORATIVE AND COOPERATIVE LEARNING STATIONS

When learning stations are set up in the classroom, students work in small groups. These students often share developments on a common display screen. This pattern follows guidelines associated with the Johnson & Johnson model (1985, 1991). Students can electronically access other students, the instructor, and learning materials. In some manner all students see the same work. This can be through a large screen monitor, projection device, or common screen shown on each student's monitor. The important feature of this classroom network is that students have connectivity and opportunities to enhance the developing product.[1]

COOPERATION AND COLLABORATION OUTSIDE THE CLASSROOM

A crucial feature of this method is the connective wiring. Communicative devices must be connected through some sort of network, telecommunication, or MODEM devices which allow sharing of data. In planning for this type of distribution and cooperation, there is no substitute for speed of transmission. Speed of transmission becomes increasingly important as video and sound become shared resources for teachers and learners.

The volume of data that can be transmitted is often expressed as "bandwidth." As networking strategies begin supporting increasingly complex multimedia applications, the bandwidth required for effective transmission increases geometrically. For example: ordinary telephone service requires a transmission speed of 2–10 Kbps (Kilobits per second). High quality compressed video requires a transmission speed of 6–24 Mbps (Megabits per second) (Hargadon 1992).[2] Transparency ECL-2 was developed to indicate to the novice the complexities of the almost geometric increases in speed and bandwidth required by new video technologies. As more and more data are transmitted faster and wider, more powerful transmission technologies are required.

TOPOLOGY

The layout (topology) of electronic networks is a special consideration for schools.

Building and campus structures often impact the network topology. Topology has important implications for the curriculum infrastructure of student networking capabilities.

- **STAR TOPOLOGY** network devices are connected by lines branching from a central node or server (Motorola Codex 1992). These "stars" radiate outward from a central location and may subdivide into other stars or "bridge" to other networks. The central node constitutes a single point of failure or maintenance. Expansion of the network does not disrupt other working devices, but transmission from outlying devices can be slowed as the network becomes larger.[3]

- **BUS OR BACKBONE TOPOLOGY** network devices are connected along a high speed, wide bandwidth central cable. These devices must be addressable (know their own address). Expansion requires no rewiring and no single node failure causes network failure (Motorola Codex 1992). [4]

- **RING OR TOKEN-RING TOPOLOGY** devices are connected in a circle. Each device acts as a repeater along the network. Control of the network is distributed, but any failure along the "ring" causes the whole network to collapse. Expansion of the network requires interruption since the ring must be temporarily broken to accommodate the installation of new nodes (Motorola Codex 1992). [5]

Few facility improvements are needed to connect to an off-site information service: computer, MODEM, phone line, and telecommunication software program. Dedicated phone lines are recommended (Eiser 1990). Planning for future installations may indicate fiberoptic networks. Fiberoptic lines have the capability of transmitting at speeds and bandwidths which will allow for full motion video.

BUDGET

The budget for electronic cooperative and collaborative learning can be as extensive or minimal as desired. For example, *FrEdMail,* started in 1984 and now serving 10,000 classrooms and 500,000 students, is free (Leslie 1993). Factors to be considered in adoption are

- Communication terminals (computers).

- Required connective devices (MODEMS, cards).

- Required wiring.

- Display devices for sharing documents.

- Specific instructor training.

- Furniture to establish collaborative and cooperative classrooms.

- Software for electronic mail or groupware.

- Telephone line charges.

- Access charges to data bases.

- Dedicated server.

TIPS-TRICKS-TRAPS

TIPS

TIP #1	One of the most effective ways of encouraging faculty use of technology and improving school communications is through electronic mail. Electronic mail not only helps the "techno-phobic" teacher get accustomed to computers, but it enhances school communication.
TIP #2	Installing a "mini-network" of computers in adjacent rooms allows students to practice cooperative and collaborative skills without meeting face to face. This strategy parallels some of the same ways business teams work on projects.
TIP #3	Develop policies and procedures for network and Internet access. These politices should address prohibited practices and penalities. Clearly publish these policies so all stake holders understand them, the reasoning behind them, and consequences of not following the outlined procedures.

TRICKS

TRICK #1	"Electronic pen pals" are a good way for students to experience foreign culture and practice language skills in foreign language classes.
TRICK #2	Networking with community resources (e.g., libraries, government agencies) provides valuable access for the school to these resources and the public can increase their use of taxpayer supported school resources.

TRAPS

TRAP #1

Schools wishing to use videotape technology with foreign students find the formats of American video (NTSC) and European video (PAL) incompatible.

TRAP #2

Schools often purchase cheaper, slower modems. The purchase of faster, higher priced modems is quickly recovered by lower telephone charges.

TRAP #3

Data transmission wiring is a technical and complex subject. Schools often purchase wiring with insufficient bandwidth to effectively transmit the data they wish to send. Schools planning for both present and anticipated networking needs may wish to contact qualified system engineers to design their school network system.

TRAP #4

Both security and the lack of security on a network can be the source of grief for school principals. A balance between "ease of use" and privacy must be planned and implemented as the network is being installed. Network security planning must involve at least three issues:

- protection from "viruses."

- unauthorized access to confidential files.

- unlawful duplication of software.

EXAMPLES

A BIOSPHERE RESEARCH EXPEDITION

Three New York junior high schools, scientific experts, and student cooperative teams were linked together by electronic mail. These collaborative groups created a research project in which they designed a life-sustaining biosphere. Students used scanners and computers to develop plans for the biosphere. They then exchanged the biosphere examples they had developed with colleagues using an electronic network. Using the same network, they critiqued colleagues' designs for scientific accuracy. The instructor felt the rewards of the program were the promotion of greater student research, student independent learning, and student networking (Reissman 1992).

LIGHTS, CAMERAS...STUDENTS

At a Florida school, teams of students were known as the "knowledge producers." These student teams got together each morning to create their own news program. This "school news program" was broadcast over the school's video system. These students didn't just watch TV; they made it. As a result of this collaboration, these students have become more aware of themselves and others. In addition to using their TV network for "school news," the students presented student dramas, interviewed guests, and gave tips on a variety of topics (Hutchins 1993).

WHAT GOT ME HOOKED

National Geographic Kids Network, an on-line network of specific lessons, brought history and geography into an elementary classroom. Students from around the world came together electronically to conduct research on timely topics including acid rain, solar energy, and water pollution. Students collected data locally and exchanged it internationally to make global connections (Novelli 1993).

BETTER TOOLS FOR BETTER TEAMWORK

A variety of technology tools were used in a classroom of mixed-ability students to help the teacher meet the needs and celebrate the strengths of all students. Learning centers were developed to foster cooperation among the students. Around these learning centers were computers, video cameras, and mini-keyboards. Students used this equipment to collaboratively author a new type of student project or product (Novelli 1993).

PEOPLE-TO-PEOPLE

"Keypals," as different from "pen pals," is a common use of wide area networking for student-to-student or group-to-group exchange. One example was a well-structured class from a suburban school in Pennsylvania. In a call for participation, a sixth grade class asked to exchange cultural information with educators and their students in foreign countries. Using *FrEdMail,* these sixth graders exchanged biographical, geographical, historical, political, social, religious, and environmental information with foreign counterparts (Harris 1994).

THE EARTH DAY TREASURE HUNT

Upper elementary and middle school students from around the country participated in a treasure hunt using telecommunications. The directors of the project had classrooms submit, by electronic mail, clues describing a geographical place. On Earth Day the clues were downloaded and students investigated a wide variety of places throughout the world. As it was an Earth Day activity, environmental clues were especially encouraged. Students were excited about developing clues for their locale and attempting to respond to the search clues provided by other students (Burry 1993).

GALAXY CLASSROOM

The schools participating in the GALAXY program set up a satellite dish, television, and FAX machine to allow students to collaborate with fellow second graders across the nation. Central to the curriculum of the GALAXY activity was a series of television dramas dealing with a variety of issues. A key component of the program was student responses using a telephone line and FAX machine. Classes and students corresponded with sister classrooms. Students often saw their work appear on subsequent issues of the television programming. Evaluation of the program found that GALAXY students' reading scores were nearly double those of control groups (Graumann 1994).

LEARNING WITH COMPUTERS

More than forty schools in several different countries participated in an international newspaper day. News articles were exchanged via electronic mail and edited into school newspapers around the world. Students spent weeks preparing the manuscripts and learning the techniques necessary to submit articles via a modem to an international network. Student excitement for the project grew as they observed their own work appearing on the international bulletin board. In one city 20,000 copies of an eight-page tabloid were printed and distributed.

Recommended Readings for Chapter 7:
Electronic Collaboration Learning

Ackerman, E. 1995. *Learning to use the internet.* Wilsonville, OR: Franklin Beedle & Associates.

Comer, D. E. 1995. *The internet.* Englewood Cliffs, NJ: Prentice Hall.

Engst, A. C. 1994. *Internet starter kit.* Indianapolis, IN: Hayden Books.

Johnson, D. W., and R. T. Johnson. 1985. Cooperative learning: One key to computer assisted learning. *The Computing Teacher 13*(1): 11–13.

Johnson, R. 1991. *Leading business teams: How teams can use technology and groups process tools to enhance performance.* Reading, MA: Addison-Wesley.

Motorola Codex. 1992. *The basics book of information networking.* Reading, MA: Addison-Wesley.

National School Boards Association. 1995. *Plans & policies for technology in education.* Alexandria, VA: National School Boards Association.

Office of Technology Assessment. 1995. *Teachers & technology: Making the connection.* Washington, D. C.: U.S. Government Printing Office.

Schrage, M. 1990. *Shared minds: The new technologies of collaboration.* New York: Random House.

Slavin, R. E. 1983. *Cooperative learning.* New York: Longman Inc.

Notes

[1] See Transparency ECL-1 for a diagram to help explain this facility modification to stakeholders.

[2] See Transparency ECL-2 for a diagram of bandwidth requirements for communication.

[3] See Transparency ECL-3 for a diagram to help explain this topography to significant stakeholders.

[4] See Transparency ECL-4 for a diagram to help explain this topography to significant stakeholders.

[5] See Transparency ECL-5 for a diagram to help explain this topography to significant stakeholders.

CHAPTER 8

Hyperlearning

*Hyperlearning is a **transformational** methodology where students are in charge of their own learning and teachers serve as guides and coaches.*

> *Everything is deeply intertwingled.*
> TED NELSON

KEY QUESTION

How can schools help students become self-directed learners to evaluate, organize, maintain, interpret, communicate, and process information electronically?

CONCEPT

Hyperlearning allows learners using electronic technologies to learn, explore, and author in nonlinear ways.

CENTER OF LEARNING CONTROL

In hyperlearning, the individual student is the center of learning control.

DISCUSSION

Hyperlearning was used by Perelman (1992) to express a view calling for the end of formal schooling. The concept of hyperlearning contains a philosophy that control of the learning process passes from the teacher to the student. This handbook recognizes schools as educational institutions, but hyperlearning environments radically alter the role of students and teachers.

Because of the difficulties in grasping hyperlearning concepts and confusion about terminology, some operational definitions have been inserted to help the reader.

> *Hypertext* (and in a broader sense Hypermedia) is a knowledge representation system composed of nodes of information on a nonlinear framework (Dede 1988).

> *Data* is input gathered by the senses (Dede 1988).

> *Information* is integrated data which denotes a significant change in the environment (Dede 1988).

Knowledge is converted information through interconnection to known concepts and skills.

Wisdom is knowledge about knowledge (Dede 1988).

Vanaver Bush (1945) and Ted Nelson (1987) envisioned technology processes where learners explored vast fields of information. In the Bush and Nelson example, each learner controlled the learning process. Recently, Thomas Armstrong (1993) related this non-linear learning model with electronic technologies to match students' cognitive strengths. Specifically, Armstrong listed in an appendix types of computer software to match individual intelligences.

Hyperlearning presumes knowledge is cross-connected in a wide array of manners (Nelson 1987). Ted Nelson's quest for "Xanadu," an electronic land where all knowledge would be accessible and interconnected, is rapidly approaching reality with the development of sophisticated web browsers on the Internet (Wolf 1995). Hyperlearning is based on a philosophy of easy access to large bodies of information (Rezabek 1989). In hyperlearning, learners are responsible for directing their own learning (Jonassen 1989). This self-directed learning imposes new responsibilities on both teachers and students. Hyperlearning has a strong background in constructivist learning theories of Piaget and Papert (1980, 1991).

Hyperlearning can take place using a print medium, for example, a thesaurus is a paper version of hypertext. However, electronic technologies have allowed explorers of any subject matter to quickly leap from topic to topic within electronic documents or information sources. Traditional methods of arranging material from beginning to end may no longer be necessary or the best way of teaching.

Because learning is centered on the learner's interests, the role of the teacher in hyperlearning changes from instructing to guiding students. Teachers are no longer the sole providers of material and direction for learning. The teacher's role becomes one of "suggester," "prompter," and "partner." This new role for teachers is different from the traditional style of dispensing predigested knowledge in a sequential, measured fashion to passive students.

PAYOFFS

Specific outcomes are difficult to measure in hyperlearning. Assessment strategies in hyperlearning are still subject to original research and debate. However, some characteristics and fields of research are encouraging. Among them are

- Hyperlearning provides easy access to huge collections of information in a variety of media.

- Hyperlearning provides students with an enabling environment rather than a directive one.

- Hyperlearning provides altered roles for teachers and students.

- Hyperlearning provides increased learner abilities in higher order thinking skills (Marchionini 1988).

STRATEGIES

In hyperlearning there are two strands: exploring and authoring. These two traits form a core for understanding hyperlearning educational strategies.

Hyperlearning exploring is when learners browse and roam through information sources seeking material interesting to them. Learners search rich data sources for chunks of information having meaning, connection, and interest. In exploring through hyperlearning environments, students construct unique meanings. In hyperlearning, a student's understanding has value because the material is connected to already acquired knowledge or experience. Students learn because it has meaning to them, not because a teacher tells them "it will be good for you." Learners build connections to material which interests them. They construct scaffolds or webs to build upon and connect to previously held knowledge.

Authoring and exploring are closely connected in hyperlearning. Because students explore in ways interesting to them, they are authoring simultaneously as they explore. In choosing pieces of data to include to make information, students have authored for themselves. Authoring in hyperlearning is exploring and exploring, in hyperlearning is authoring.

MULTIMEDIA–EXPLORING

Multimedia is a strategy often associated with hyperlearning. The term "hypermedia" is used to connote *hyper*text and multi*media*. "Hyper" implies nonlinear. Multimedia denotes the use of many media forms of communication: sound, animation, video, graphics, and still images. As a strategy, learners create or interact with nonlinear projects and demonstrate their understanding through the use of multimedia. *Odysseys* © (IBM) is an example of hypermedia. In this project, learners explore Homer's epic poem in a non-linear fashion using text, sound, graphics, and video.

HYPERTEXT–EXPLORING

Hypertext is usually, but not always, an electronic document for individual learner exploration. These documents contain a variety of media: text, graphics, sound, etc. Learners leap from one section to another depending on their particular interests. A useful paper example may be a student browsing an encyclopedia, following paths unique to his or her own interests. Electronic hypertext exploring is shown by *Culture*© (Cultural Resources) or *Timeline*© (MECC) or *The First Emperor of China*©(Voyager). In these examples, students explore electronic text documents linking art, music, and history.

HYPERLEARNING–EXPLORING VIA NETWORK

If connected by a MODEM and phone line, learners interested in their own discovery can access immense sources of information. From these resources, they gather data suitable for their own learning. They have the power to use these sources of information to create an understanding for themselves and knowledge for others. This strategy was visioned by Ted Nelson (1987) in *Xanadu* and is practiced by learners searching both publicly owned networks (e.g., *INTERNET*) and commercial networks (e.g., *Prodigy®*).

HYPERLEARNING–AUTHORING

Learners author nonlinear documents, using either text or media. These documents express their understanding, but allow for a variety of "reader" interest. Authoring tools for this process are *HyperCard©* (Claris), *Linkway Live©* (IBM), *HyperStudio®* (Roger Wagner), and *Guide©* (Owl). These authoring tools are more than word processors. They gain their power from their ability to connect nodes of information by associative links. Moreover, these programs use other electronic documents, such as laser disks, to present data and information in an interactive way. If electronically connected to other hyperlearners, authors can collaboratively develop hyperlearning documents.

The teacher's role in a hypertextual learning environment changes as radically as the student's role. Rather than addressing students from a position as "sage on the stage," teachers become "guides on the side." Rather than the source of all learning, teachers are counselors in student exploration of the vast field of knowledge. The teacher's role is to aid students in reflection about their own learning. Teachers engaging in hyperlearning methods must develop a new set of highly sophisticated skills. These skills include a broader and deeper understanding of subject domains, new skills in questioning, suggesting paths for exploration, and helping students construct their own understanding.

Jonassen (1986) noted learner control is based on two assumptions: 1) learners know what is best for them at any given time and 2) learners are capable of acting appropriately on this knowledge. The teacher's role becomes one of enabling learners to fulfill these two assumptions.

What would teachers' use of hyperlearning methods look like?

- Nontraditional methods of evaluation, which include electronic portfolios, standards negotiated between "coach" and "student," evaluation based on learner reflection.

- Learners developing their own goals for learning.

• Teachers as "guides on the side."

STUDENTS

The student role in a hyperlearning methodology is significantly different from past educational methods. Rather than acting as passive recipients of information flowing from teacher to student, students become active participants in creating their own learning. In advanced hyperlearning methods, individual students determine what to explore, what knowledge interests them, what medium of expression suits their intelligence, and in what time frame they want it presented. Empowerment for students becomes a real possibility for student-directed learning.

Empowerment of students in hyperlearning methods challenges many fundamental assumptions of reforms calling for greater uniformity and standards of educational accomplishment. The material to be examined is determined by the student. The standards for success are accomplished not in relationship to national norms, but in relationship to the needs of the student and future employers. This new found freedom of students to explore and develop their own learning contains a heavy responsibility. Student directed learning provokes new standards for evaluation which include student self-assessment, electronic portfolios, and demonstration projects.

What would students' use of hyperlearning technology methods look like?

- A new, nonlinear method of authoring.

- Technical skills involving multimedia.

- Increased enthusiasm for student-directed learning.

- Learning attached to students' previously known material.

- Inquisitive exploration of topics by students.

- Students' examination of their own learning process.

FACILITIES

Schools seeking to institute hyperlearning models in their buildings usually find specific facility requirements to be less of a problem than with other technology-based learning methods. Hypertext and hypermedia are more a state of mind than a concrete structural development. Hyperlearning relies more on attitudes about student centered learning than a large investment in equipment or facilities. These practices can be initiated on an experimental basis with little room modification.

Hyperlearning can make advantageous use of other technological developments requiring extensive facilities modification. However, extensive facility modification is not required. One stand alone computer with a minimum of software and enthusiastic teachers and students is the start of hyperlearning. Specialized equipment for this type of instruction includes:

HYPERTEXT:

- Computer.

- Specialized software.

HYPERMEDIA:

- Computer

- Equipment for multimedia (e.g., video, laser disk audio, graphic, CD-ROM, etc.).

BUDGET

The budget for hyperlearning is small compared with other technology applications. The budget is small because equipment required and facilities modification are minimal. Depending upon the computer platform selected by the school district one or two software packages can start a hyperlearning program.

TIPS-TRICKS-TRAPS

TIPS

TIP #1

Teachers should establish clearly negotiated goals for student projects at the start of the project development. This avoids confusion and acrimony at the end of the project.

TIP #2

Teachers should involve parents at the outset of a hyperlearning project to enlist their support and insure they clearly understand the goals and purposes of the project.

TIP #3

Teachers should initiate a public relations effort with the media about new learning strategies involving hyperlearning. If the community and significant stakeholders are unclear about the goals and techniques of hyperlearning at the start of such a project, rumors can develop that students are just "doing their own thing" while the teachers no longer teach.

TIP #4

Allow plenty of time for exploration. Students cannot connect the associated links that make hyperlearning powerful in pressured time frames. They must have time to search many sources, develop and discard many ideas, and select the meaningful bits of information that assemble into an informed whole.

TRICKS

TRICK #1

Students practice writing hyperlearning with flow charts, storyboards, and different endings to fairy tales. At a young age, students can start to explore authoring in a nonlinear fashion. Traditional writing practice has been linear.

TRICK #2

Instructors are thoroughly trained in both the electronic skills and new roles as "guides on the side." Key to this trick is training teachers to use new methods of instruction and to perceive new roles for themselves in the teaching and learning process. Basic technical skill in new equipment is insufficient for the change in attitude and practice that must accompany this equipment for effective hyperlearning to take place.

TRICK #3

Workshops and activities for the faculty on constructivist philosophies and learning techniques are scheduled. Faculty must be made aware of recent advances in constructivist learning and cognitive psychology.

TRICK #4

Faculty and students can investigate assessment of hyperlearning products in ways similar to ways traditional essays are assessed. At the same time, new assessment strategies for hyperlearning products must be explored by teachers and students.

Web browsers such as Mosaic® and Netscape® provide excellent examples of hyperlearning environments on networks. Text and graphics have associated links to other information sources for students to explore.

TRAPS

Without strong guidance, hyperlearning projects lack meaningful substance. Because traditional methods of assessment are meaningless in hyperlearning, new forms of assessment must be carefully crafted at the outset.

Measuring student achievement from hyperlearning projects with traditional standardized testing is destined for failure.

LEARNING BEYOND THE CLASSROOM

Students, teachers, and parents established a high technology network of computers, multimedia imaging equipment, and satellite technology to link the school with many information resources. They studied science, world history, politics, and current events by investigating resources linked to this network. Students were able to access and retrieve video programs and filmstrips through a school-based technology resource center. Teachers were able to create their own CD-Interactive disks for classroom instruction (Electronic Learning, 1993).

MATHEMATICAL EXPLORATION IN LOGO

A pilot study of sixth-grade students engaged in mathematical explorations was carried out in the context of a national LOGO project in Costa Rica. Thirty-four students, approximately twelve years old, worked in pairs investigating a mathematical microworld written in LOGO. The investigation had three phases: 1) open exploration of the microworld, during which the students recorded their observations and formulated hypotheses about how the program worked; 2) group discussion and sharing of hypothesis; and 3) additional guided discovery and problem-solving. The students were successful in discovering certain functions of their microworld during the first phase, but their hypotheses were improved after discussion with the instructor. The students were successful in applying their knowledge of the computer microworld in problem-solving tasks during the third phase (Edwards 1994).

HISTORY COMES ALIVE

Using *HyperCard,* a school district began to store information about the culture, language, and history of a local Native American tribe. Before the project was completed the school was selling CD-ROM copies of the "Culture and History of the White Earth Ojibwe" for $20.00. The menu for exploration of this CD-ROM project included options for K–6 social studies, 7–9 social studies, natural resources, Native American poetry, language arts, Ojibwe leaders, Native American foods, civics, and classroom champions (Sterns 1993).

LINKWAY FEATURES AND DESIGN

In a effort to help students clarify and define problems, students from San Francisco worked on the following problem:

> *Transportation is a matter of concern, especially in urban areas where growth is taking place. As a result of the 1989 Loma Preita earthquake, a major artery through San Francisco, the Embarcadero Freeway, was closed, causing traffic congestion, as well as making Chinatown less accessible to tourists. Should the freeway be rebuilt?*

Students engaged searched files of the *San Francisco Chronicle* and *San Jose Mercury.* These databases were found on Dialog's CLASSMATE service. From their first set of articles, students formulated specific search questions involving the reconstruction of the freeway. In this online search activity, students focused on finding answers to real-life problems (Abramson 1993).

Recommended Readings for Chapter 8: Hyperlearning

Bevilacqua, A. F. 1989. *Hypertext: Behind the hype.* (ERIC Document Reproduction Service No. ED 308 882).

Bush, V. 1945. The way we may think. *The Atlantic 176*(1):101–8.

Dede, C. 1987. Empowering environments, hypermedia and microworlds. *The Computing Teacher 15*(3): 20–24.

———. 1988. *The role of hypertext in transforming information into knowledge.* NECC Conference, Dallas, TX, 1988.

Jonassen, D. H. 1989. *Hypertext/Hypermedia.* Englewood Cliffs, NJ: Educational Technology Publications.

Nelson, T. 1987. *Computer lib/dream machines.* Redmond, WA: Microsoft Press.

Papert, S. 1980. *Mindstorms: Children, computers, and powerful ideas.* New York: Basic Books.

———. 1993. *The children's machine: Rethinking school in the age of the computer.* New York: Basic Books.

Papert, S., and I. Harel, eds. 1991. *Constructionism.* Norwood, NJ: Ablex.

Perelman, L. J. 1992. *School's out: Hyperlearning, the new technology, and the end of education.* New York: William Morrow and Company.

CHAPTER 9

Electronic Learning Simulations

*Electronic learning simulation is a **restructuring** methodology where technology is used to create electronic learning scenarios.*

> *Everything is curiouser and curiourser.*
>
> LEWIS CARROLL
> *ALICE IN WONDERLAND*

KEY QUESTION

How can schools, using technology, help students understand systems for improving and correcting performance?

CONCEPT

In electronic learning simulations, students acquire concepts and understandings by interacting with scenarios produced by emerging electronic devices.

CENTER OF LEARNING CONTROL

The center of learning control is jointly held by the learner(s) and the computer.

DISCUSSION

Electronic simulation is an educational process where students react to situations presented by software programing. These situations are designed to mirror real-life scenarios. Well-executed simulations provide a sense of life experience and learning occurs through fundamental change in attitude and behavior (Henderson 1991). Electronic simulation involves computing in a choice-laden environment. Electronic simulation often includes multimedia.

How does electronic simulation differ from other types of Computer Assisted Instruction (CAI)? CAI instruction involves students in learning detailed, decontextualized segments of information (e.g., math facts, states and state capitals, periodic table).

In electronic simulations, the learner makes decisions that affect the outcome of the simulation. Success or failure within the simulation is dependent not upon student learning a series of specific facts, but upon the student ability to react and make choices from the responses relayed to them by the equipment.

Computer simulations for education imitate complex real-world situations. A common use in educational environments is for social studies and physical sciences. In social science students often "act" out historical roles. In science they explore complex behavior of objects in Newtonian environments. These representations have been difficult to grasp by other means (O.T.A. 1988).

Visionaries see electronic simulations expanding into a new convergence of technologies (McLellan 1991; Traub 1991) called virtual reality. Virtual reality, a future extension of electronic simulation, is not yet practical or cost effective for schools. Business, entertainment, and the military make great use of virtual reality and it will soon become available to schools (Reveaux 1992). Principals may wish to keep up-to-date on virtual reality as it allows learners to enter computer-simulated, three-dimensional environments (Helsel 1992; Hill 1992; McClellan 1991; Perelman 1992).

PAYOFFS

Teachers have difficulty documenting specific learning growth from electronic learning simulations with traditional methods of assessment. An electronic simulation may have a definite lesson to be learned (e.g., the pioneers' difficulties, the effects of cutting down the rain forest, or the results of economic policy designs). The objectives may be cognitive. The objectives may be affective. The growth of each learner working with the simulation is difficult to document. Not all learners come away from the simulation with the same experience. If the simulation allows multiple paths and solutions, different learners will solve the problem different ways. Most current test instruments are not designed to measure many different understandings.

Some payoffs may appear that are not "measurable" by standardized tests. Among these may be

- Enthusiasm for learning by "playing a game."

- A greater depth of understanding by accessing several senses.

- An affective understanding of complex topics studied by simulation.

- A systems perspective through role-playing in simulations.

STRATEGIES

SINGLE-LEARNER SIMULATION

Social studies class members take turns at the computer exploring, learning, and investigating with a simulation that matches the curriculum. Some popular programs for this strategy are *Oregon Trail©* (MECC), which investigates the difficulties of pioneers, and *Where in the World is Carmen Sandiego?©* (Broderbund), which takes students on a hunt for an arch-villain with clues from world geography.

In science, *Interactive Physics II©* (Knowledge Revolution) provides students with computer environments to simulate realistic motion. Using this program, students investigate planetary motion that may take years to occur. *Interactive Physics II©* allows students to perform experiments in zero gravity situations.

LEARNING-TEAM SIMULATION

Learners work in teams to solve problems generated by computer simulations. These simulations are often current social or environmental problems which present learners with the difficulties faced by real world decision makers. Some examples are *SimCity©* and *SimEarth©* (Broderbund).

Faculty understanding of electronic simulation is just now coming to the front. Role-playing activities have been with education for some time. However, the power to access a wide variety of branches in any solution or develop new options leaves faculty members searching for educational applications of this new technology. In addition, assessment of educational accomplishment may be different for students who have availed themselves of different paths in the simulation.

What would staff members' use of electronic learning simulations look like?

- Incorporation of electronic simulation into the curriculum.

- Authentic learning experiences for students using electronic simulations.

- Students, through electronic simulation, learning complex psycho-motor skills which are dangerous or difficult to recreate in the real world.

- Electronic simulations reinforce and create new understandings of curriculum objectives.

STUDENTS

Learners in simulation activities understand a wide range of events. The learners develop a greater understanding of the complex interrelationships involved with science and social science.

What would students' use of electronic learning simulations look like?

- Deeper, empathetic understanding of course material.

- Improved decision-making skills.

- Improved collaborative skills.

- Improved psycho-motor skills.

- Cooperative efforts to solve complex, real-life simulations.

FACILITIES

Schools planning facilities for electronic simulations need only provide a computer, display screen, and a cart to carry this equipment.

Specialized equipment for simulation includes

- Computer.

- Specialized software.

BUDGET

Schools possessing relatively modern computer equipment find the cost of simulation software packages moderate. Many of these packages need little additional investment in hardware or staff training.

TIPS-TRICKS-TRAPS

TIPS

TIP #1

Students enjoy playing games. Electronic simulations often appear to be games in the eyes of students. Electronic simulations can be an exciting way to accomplish learning objectives.

TIP #2

Effective educators harness the competitiveness of students using electronic simulations. Teaming is an effective tactic. Teachers should insure all students of all abilities have equal opportunity for success either individually or as part of a team.

TIP #3

Adventure games provides excellent opportunities for simulation to develop thinking skills. Students using adventure games can work in fantasy worlds or computer simulations of real worlds that offer them opportunities to explore and test a variety of problem-solving strategies.

TRICKS

TRICK #1

Many simulations work well on equipment that is becoming out-of-date. Electronic simulations can often use this older equipment to reinforce and enhance the curriculum.

TRICK #2

Electronic simulations often imitate arcade style "games" with sound, animation, and regular reinforcement.

TRAPS

TRAP #1

Often simulations are used for reward and are unrelated to the curriculum. This is easy to spot. Students are using an electronic simulation for topics not being covered in the regular program of students. This leads to parental concerns about the kids just playing games at school rather than learning.

TRAP #2

Some electronic simulations take hours to evolve. Given traditional time restraints in class, beware of such simulations. Also, because of their length they may not be able to sustain student interest.

Choosing an electronic simulation with motivational sound and graphics unsuitable to the age level of students can have a detrimental effect on student interest.

SCORE

Penn State University, with funding from AT&T, designed courseware for developing industry-specific skills for adults. The emphasis was on "mid-literate" adults who needed additional training in basic skills. The courseware (SCORE) used simulations in a functional context to teach basic skills. Each simulation was in a highly visual scenario. Workers arrived at their "simulated" work space, did the job, and received evaluation on their performance from a "simulated" supervisor. SCORE taught basic workplace skills in math, reading, writing, problem solving, and critical thinking. Learners in this simulation sometimes worked together in small groups to enhance teamwork and communication skills. At other times they worked individually (Bixler & Spotts 1994).

SAVE THE CITIES!

Using the "game" *SimCity©*, twenty-four gifted students in a pull-out instructional program were introduced to an aspect of life they could not have experienced in a small town on a remote island of Alaska. They were introduced to the effects of decisions made by major metropolitan politicians. After a general "walk-through" of the program *SimCity©* by the teacher, the students were turned loose to "run" their simulated cities. Elementary school students were presented with the need to make critical, controversial decisions concerning taxes and city services (Jacobson 1992).

PUTTING LIFE INTO COMPUTER-BASED TRAINING

"Outbreak: Pharyngitis in Louisiana," provides a realistic computer-based case study to simulate a disease outbreak in which students played the role of lead investigator. This simulation, developed by the Center for Disease Control and Prevention, allowed investigators to perform a variety of tasks related to the outbreak of a major disease threat. The major thrust of this simulation was to teach students how to conduct disease outbreak investigations. In the development of this simulation, three techniques were used to insure the simulations reflected real life as much as possible: realistic content portrayals, engaging graphics, and interactive teaching methods. Multiple outcomes were possible depending upon the choices made during the course of the simulation (Gathany & Stehr-Green 1994).

OUTSIDE, A WORLD GOES BY

Using *Microsoft Flight Simulator,* twelve- to sixteen-year-old students simulated real world navigation problems using math skills they learned during regular instruction. This classroom simulation solidified what they already new and taught them to recognize the importance of the information and skills acquired during math. Students were encouraged to work as teams or whole classes on the simulated flights. A few advanced students were allowed to increase their skills and abilities in a simulation of their own. Commonly, students were asked to determine speed, time, distance, direction, and altitude in a group effort (Van Den Brink 1994).

VIRTUAL BACKHOE

Beckman Institute for Advanced Science at the University of Illinois, developed one of the first projects in virtual reality in a lab to develop skills in the operation of a backhoe. Trainees in backhoe operation had a virtual world displayed for them. This simulated world was analogous to the actual operation of a backhoe. The technological equipment involved in the virtual reality simulation allowed for portrayal of "actual" sight and sounds of backhoe operation. The sights were provided through the use of multiple cameras. The sound was conveyed through stereo headphones (NCSA Applications 1994).

VIRTUAL REALITY LANDS THE JOB

When the Hubble Telescope failed to live up to its planned performance, the National Aeronautics and Space Administration set out on an ambitious plan to repair the telescope in space. In order to simulate the difficulties anticipated in such a complex operation, the repairs were practiced in a virtual reality simulation at the Johnson Space Center. Each trainee wore a head-mounted display and an input glove. The simulator allowed movement around a simulated space shuttle payload bay as though the trainee was in space. The director of the project said the virtual reality simulation helped those who would repair the shuttle understand procedures and equipment much better than traditional books, models, and diagrams (Delaney 1994).

WHERE IN THE WORLD

Sixth-grade students used *Where in the World Is Carmen Sandiego?©* as a simulation to help develop thinking skills. The students were grouped and given several sessions to play the adventure game. They recorded on a word processor all the clues they encountered. Over a thousand clues were collected and sorted into categories for printing. This database was also made available on a disk and students were taught basic commands and how to retrieve information from a database. The students learned research skills in addition to learning how to use word processors and a database. Their efforts were later shared with the entire school.

Recommended Readings for Chapter 9:
Electronic Learning Simulations

Helsel, S. K. 1990. *Interactive optical technologies in education and training.* Westport, CT: Meckler.

————. 1992. Virtual reality as a learning medium. *Instructional Delivery Systems* 6(4): 4–5.

Henderson, J. 1991. Designing realities: Interactive media, virtual realities and cyberspace. In S. K. Helsel and J. P. Roth, eds. *Virtual reality: Theory, practice and promise.* Meckler: Westport, CT.

Lantz, E. 1992. Virtual reality in science museums, *Instructional Delivery Systems* 6(4): 10–12.

Perelman, L. J. 1992. *School's out: Hyperlearning, the new technology, and the end of education.* New York: William Morrow and Company.

PART III

Implementing Technology-Based Learning

CHAPTER 10

Technology Adoption Model

*The technology adoption model
provides a step-by-step process for
implementing selected technology-
based learning methods.*

KEY QUESTIONS

Is there a model or pattern to aid in the implementation process of technology-based learning methods?

How in a step-by-step process do technology leaders go about installing chosen technology-based learning methods?

This section is devoted to providing a model for installing a selected technology-based learning method (TLM). Stakeholders may select one or more technology-based learning methods for their school. In pursuit of their educational goals. Stakeholders choose learning methods and appropriate strategies for teachers and students. The essential question is how, in a step-by-step process, do schools set about installing a chosen TLM in their building? This section provides a model to answer that question.

A DECISION MAKING FLOW CHART: TECHNOLOGY ADOPTION MODEL (TAM)

KEY QUESTION

How do schools go about installing selected TLM in their building?

The T(echnology) A(doption) M(odel) (see Figure 4) helps technology leaders or technology teams see the process for installing a new technology-based learning method. The process outlined by the TAM begins with investigation of a technology-based learning method (TLM) and ends at the beginning with investigation of another TLM for adoption. The TAM diagrams these decisions along with several "stop points" throughout the implementation process.

These "stop points" halt the progress toward district implementation at that level. Decisions involving "stop" do not necessarily indicate abandonment of the technology-based learning method. A "stop point" may be for modification of that method at that level. At a "stop point," technology leaders or planning teams may decide to implement the technology-based learning method at only their level, while other technology leaders and their planning teams may choose different technology-based learning methods.

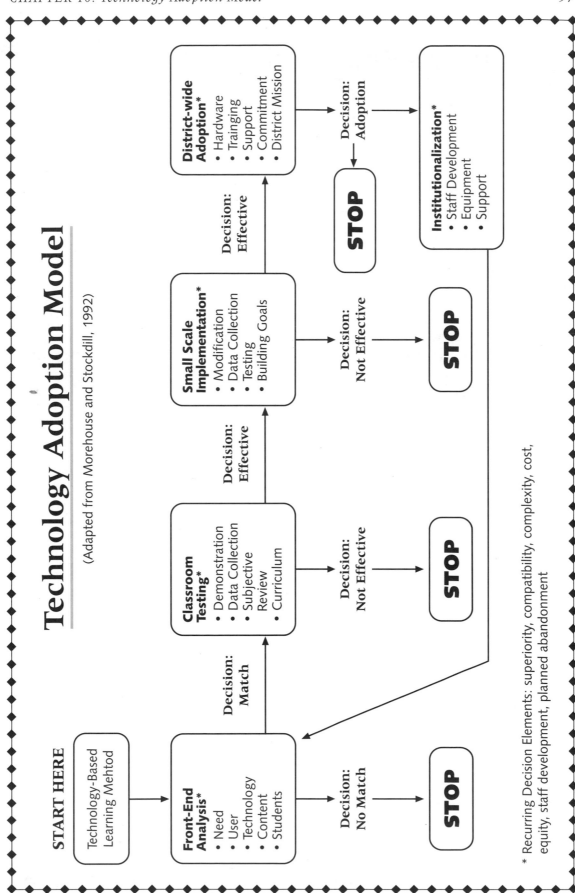

Technology Adoption Model

(Adapted from Morehouse and Stockdill, 1992)

START HERE

Technology-Based Learning Mehtod

Front-End Analysis*
• Need
• User
• Technology
• Content
• Students

Decision: No Match → **STOP**

Decision: Match →

Classroom Testing*
• Demonstration
• Data Collection
• Subjective Review
• Curriculum

Decision: Not Effective → **STOP**

Decision: Effective →

Small Scale Implementation*
• Modification
• Data Collection
• Testing
• Building Goals

Decision: Not Effective → **STOP**

Decision: Effective →

District-wide Adoption*
• Hardware
• Trainging
• Support
• Commitment
• District Mission

Decision: Adoption →

STOP

Institutionalization*
• Staff Development
• Equipment
• Support

* Recurring Decision Elements:: superiority, compatibility, complexity, cost, equity, staff development, planned abandonment

Figure 4

RECURRING DECISION ELEMENTS OF THE TAM

KEY QUESTION

What decisions must be made for any Technology-based Learning Method?

There are seven recurring decision elements in each stage of the TAM. They are superiority, compatibility, cost, complexity, equity, staff development, and planned abandonment. Each of these recurring decision elements of the TAM poses specific questions to be addressed by those interested in technological implementation. Schools seeking to effectively install TLMs in their educational settings positively respond to questions concerning the superiority, compatibility, complexity, cost, equity, and staff development of the TLM.

SUPERIORITY

Is this technology-based learning method and its accompanying strategies *superior* to instructional methods currently in place or to other methods which could be chosen?

COMPATIBILITY

Is this technology-based learning method *compatible* with the goals and aspirations of this school? Does this technology-based learning method match with other learning methods and strategies of the school?

COMPLEXITY

Is the *complexity* of the technology-based learning method, accompanying strategies, and equipment at a level which can be mastered by those who will be using the learning method?

COST

Is this technology-based learning method *cost effective?* Could the same amount of money provide greater returns in student accomplishment if applied elsewhere?

EQUITY

Is this technology-based learning method *equitable* in the way it treats all groups within the student population: gender, race, handicap, culture, or socioeconomic level?

STAFF DEVELOPMENT

Is there, or will there be, sufficient *staff development* for those involved in the technology-based learning method to insure its effective implementation in the classroom? Are both skill training and classroom applications addressed in the staff development plans for this technology-based learning method? Because of the critical nature of staff development for technology, Chapter 11 has been devoted to this issue.

PLANNED ABANDONMENT

Have plans been made for the *abandonment* of old teaching and learning practices that will be replaced by the technology-based learning method?

USING THE TAM THROUGH SIX STAGES

KEY QUESTION

How is the TAM Used?

STAGE 1
Technology-based Learning Method

Appropriate members of the technology planning team start by selecting a learning method which addresses the need of their school building. A group of "technology-wise" administrators and teachers may need to "blaze the trail" in order to establish "needs awareness" on the part of the staff. The chosen TLM may be teacher-centered, Integrated Learning System, electronic collaboration, hyperlearning, or electronic simulation.

STAGE 2
Front-End Analysis

In addition to the recurring decision elements, the technology planning team seeks to answer five questions in this stage of the TAM (Review Figure 4).

1. Is there a *need* for this technology-based learning method?

2. Are there *users* on the staff who would profitably employ this technology-based learning method?

3. Is there *technology* sufficient to carry out this technology-based learning method?

4. Is the curriculum *content* amenable to this technology-based learning method?

5. Does this technology-based learning method suit the needs of the *students?*

STAGE 3
Classroom Testing

In addition to the recurring decision elements, the technology planning team seeks to answer four questions at this stage of the TAM.

1. Where can we find or create a classroom *demonstration* project for this technology-based learning method?

2. What *data* supports the installation of this technology-based learning method?

3. What have been the *subjective reviews* of this technology-based learning method?

4. Does this technology-based learning method enhance the building *curriculum?*

STAGE 4
Small Scale Implementation

In addition to the recurring decision elements, the technology planning team seeks to answer five questions in this stage of the TAM.

1. What *modification* is necessary for further implementation of the technology-based learning method?

2. Has *data collection* supported the goals of this technology-based learning method?

3. What sort of *testing* adequately reviews this technology-based learning method?

4. Is this technology-based learning method compatible with the overall *building goals?*

5. Is this technology-based learning method compatible with the *subject goals* in the applicable course of study?

STAGE 5
District-wide Adoption

In addition to the recurring decision elements, the technology planning team seeks to answer five questions in this stage of the TAM.

1. Is the *hardware* available for district-wide installation of this technology-based learning method?

2. Can sufficient *training* for this technology-based learning method be assured?

3. Can adequate *support* for this technology-based learning method be assured?

4. Is there a long term *commitment* for this technology-based learning method.

5. Is this technology-based learning method compatible with the *district mission?*

STAGE 6
Institutionalization

The final stage in this six part flow chart focuses on three questions for effective institutionalization of a technology-based learning method.

1. Is sufficient, quality *staff development* planned to insure the district-wide institutionalization of the chosen technology-based learning method?

2. Is sufficient *equipment* available to insure the district-wide institutionalization of the chosen technology-based learning method?

3. Is sufficient *support* available to insure the district-wide institutionalization of the chosen technology-based learning method?

Following the completion of the sixth stage of the TAM, the process begins again with investigation of a new TLM or the application of the same TLM to a different content area.

Recommended Readings for Chapter 10: Technology Adoption Model

Apple Computer Inc. 1991. *Teaching, learning & technology: A planning guide.* Cupertino, CA: Apple Corporation.

Bailey, G. D., and D. Lumley. 1994. *Technology staff development programs: A leadership sourcebook for school administrators.* New York: Scholastic, Inc.

Center for Learning Technologies. 1984. *Getting started: Planning and implementing computer instruction in schools.* Albany, NY: Center for Learning Technologies.

Dede, C. 1989. Planning guidelines for emerging instructional technologies. *Educational Technology* 29(4): 7–12.

Lumley, D., and G. D. Bailey. 1993. *Planning for technology: A guidebook for school administrators.* New York: Scholastic, Inc.

Morehouse, D. E., and S. H. Stockdill. 1992. Technology adoption model. *Educational Technology* 32(2): 57–59.

Professional Development

This chapter provides a brief survey for implementing a staff development program for technology-based learning. In this chapter is a four-stage model for technology staff development.

KEY QUESTIONS

What can technology leaders do to effectively implement staff development for technology-based learning?

What kind of staff development program is necessary to successfully implement change in how teachers use the emerging technologies to engage students?

Staff development for technology is the crucial factor facing those who want to bring about technology-based learning methods. A brief outline of strategies is provided in this chapter. This outline is not a substitute for a thorough, fully articulated and shared staff development program.

THE ROCKET OF STAFF DEVELOPMENT

An effective staff development program for technology depends on four convergent factors occuring at the same place and the same time. These four factors are much like the ingredients that combine in rocket engines to propel space craft. These four factors are skills, resources, vision, and incentives. Skills, resources, vision, and incentives must all be brought together at the same time for an effective technology staff development program to take off. If any one factor is absent and aborted, takeoff is unlikely.

RESOURCES

Staff members learning to use technology progams and equipment in the classroom must have ready access to the equipment when they return to their regular stations from a staff development progam. If teachers are taught how to use equipment they will not have, they have no reason to learn the skill and no opportunity to practice it. Without such resources, the "rocket of staff development" lacks fuel.

SKILLS

Staff development leaders must be able to demonstrate the skills they are advocating. They must be able to "walk the talk." They must have the ability to impart their skills to the participants of the staff development program. To talk about how to use technology without being able to demonstrate its use in the classroom is not sufficient. Without such skills, the "rocket of staff development" lacks control.

VISION

The leaders of the staff development programs must have a clear vision of technology and technology's implications for the world and the classroom. Without such a vision, the "rocket of staff development" lacks direction.

INCENTIVES

Staff development leaders must provide rewards and incentives for those involved in technology development. Teachers must know their efforts are appreciated and supported by members of the administrative team and district governance. To ask staff members to embark on the difficult task of incorporating technology into new learning methods requires rewards. Without such incentives, the "rocket of staff development" lacks riders.

Outstanding technology leaders are able to provide these four components in the right amounts at the right time. It is a complex skill—almost an art—to provide technology staff development and avoid the syndrome of "too much, too soon; too little too late." Effective technology staff development for teachers brings the four factors of skills, resources, vision, and incentives together in an "on time, on target" program.

Finally, staff development for technology must be on-going for the "rocket" to continue soaring. Withdraw any of the four factors and the "rocket" sputters and dies for a lack of propelling ingredients. Technology staff development is on-going and continuous. It is not a "one shot deal." "One shot" programs provide much noise and smoke, but the rocket crashes shortly after leaving the launch pad.

A FOUR-STAGE PLAN

A thorough treatment of staff development programs for integrating technology into education is found in *Technology Staff Development Programs—A Leadership Sourcebook for School Administrators* (1994) by Gerald Bailey and Dan Lumley. In this handbook, managing the complexity of a staff development for implementing the various teaching methodologies is divided into four stages.

STAGE 1: Prepare for change.

STAGE 2: Plan the program.

STAGE 3: Implement the program.

STAGE 4: Institutionalize the program.

The technology leader can use these four stages to prepare faculty for experimenting and exploring various technology-based learning methods.

STAGE 1
Prepare for Change

Instructional staff and other members involved in technology must understand the change process relative to emerging technologies. The change process requires having a vision. Technology leaders must have and provide skills, incentives, resources, and plans to implement the vision. Effective technology staff development programs prepare teachers for the change process and provide ownership in the vision for transforming schools.

In addition, teachers need to recognize there are three different competencies found in professional development programs:

1. Knowledge—having an understanding of information.

2. Attitudes—values or opinions related to the technology-based learning methods.

3. Skills—specific behaviors which permit teachers to use emerging technologies to construct major learning methods.

Teachers also must recognize that emerging technologies include a wide range of electronic technologies which are used to enhance teaching and learning. These include computer, interactive videodisc, CD-ROM, videotape, audiotape, television, facsimile transmission (FAX), telephone, modem, robotics, and virtual reality.

Discussions focusing on these emerging technologies and how they can be used in creating various technology-based learning methods is the first stage of an effective technology staff development program. Essential to these discussions is the meaning of the terms school reform, school restructuring, and school transformation (See Preface).

STAGE 2
Plan the Program

Staff development is a key aspect of the Technology Adoption Model in Chapter 10. Staff involvement in the design and implementation of technology programs is imperative. An effective technology staff development program creates leadership committees at both the district and building level to help craft the technology staff development program. The creation of two committees is important because staff development must occur both top-down as well as bottom-up. In essence, elements of the district technology staff development program need to insure that district personnel as well as building personnel understand and are skilled at using the technology. Leadership must be exerted simultaneously at both levels for effective technology staff development programs.

The building principal is a key technology leader in the building technology staff development committee. The building principal as technology leader should exhibit a variety of technology leadership skills. The building leader, in crafting this program, should give careful consideration to involving key players impacted by the technology staff development program. These key players include the superintendent, school board members, parents, support staff, substitute teachers, media/library specialists, as well as the primary user of the technology-based learning methodologies—the classroom teacher.

Careful use of audits can provide valuable information when planning technology staff develop programs. The information gathered from the audits can be used to fashion guiding documents in the form of a mission statement, goals, and action plan. With a well crafted plan in place, training in the technology-based learning methods can begin.

Without a written plan, technology staff development lacks direction. The written plan must identify the vision, skills, incentives, resources, and plan of action. With this in mind, implementation of technology staff development programs begins.

STAGE 3
Implement the Program

Specific elements of the technology-based learning methods training program should begin to explore the following concepts with regard to the technology-based methods:

1. Teachers as guide-on-the side, mentor, co-learner, evaluator, and co-evaluator.

2. Basic literacy and information literacy (see preface for a definition of information literacy).

Six basic principles should guide technology leaders as they consider how to deliver the technology staff development program:

1. No single delivery system is sufficient or "right" in any one technology staff development program.

2. Technology-based learning methodologies need to be explored and used as participants are trained.

3. Most program gains and participant breakthroughs are made by allowing people to work in teams.

4. Teams should be provided time to think, reflect, and dream.

5. Combining or offering alternative learning methods offers a more powerful learning environment than relying exclusively on **one** TLM.

6. Participants usually have preferences of how to learn; therefore, participants should have a choice in selecting one or more technology-based learning systems to learn about.

ACTIVITIES

There are a variety of activities that should be considered:

1. Have teams brainstorm about possible emerging technologies that could be used in TLMs.

2. Identify other schools or business that are using TLMs. Visit these locations. Videotape and allow committees to study and critique TLMs in action.

3. Have teachers and administrators model one or more TLMs for others to watch, videotape, and critique.

4. Allow for and encourage a great deal of experimentation with the methodologies. Underscore the importance of experimentation without punishment or public embarrassment.

LEARNING TEAMS

The creation of learning teams as a major form of staff development is important. The learning cycle in mastering the technology-based methods should be considered in the training process. A training cycle includes four basic steps (1) information, (2) demonstration, (3) practice, and (4) feedback and coaching.

Step 1

Team members are exposed to and share information. A period of time that is set aside to absorb new information and discuss the TLMS.

Step 2

Team members schedule opportunities for watching each other or others who are demonstrating the TLM.

Step 3

Team members practice the behavior that has been previously discussed and observed. After practicing, team members can schedule a meeting to share their experiences and discuss their feelings and attitudes.

Step 4

Team members ask for feedback and begin the coaching process. Coaching helps other team members master the skills found in the TLMs.

CRITICAL CONSIDERATIONS

Consider the Physical Environment

Physical environment includes those things such as chairs, lighting, wall color, space, and air flow. The bottom line is that the physical environment must provide for all those things which are going to be used back in the classroom.

Consider Incentives

There needs to be a wide range of incentives offered to participants. The bottom line is that there must be a variety of ways to motivate staff.

Consider Creature Comforts

Creature comforts can be defined as any food that is provided to participants or brought by participants. It has been said that armies march on their stomachs. If this is true, then staff developers are no different. Food and social interaction are natural and necessary in technology staff development programs.

Consider Plug-in Environment and Hot-line Help

Participants need to feel that the equipment requires little preparation for use and that they have access to someone who can operate and explain the equipment and its purpose. If overlooked, these two crucial elements portend difficulties for technology staff development programs. (See Figure 5, "20 Rules for Effective Technology Staff Development.")

STAGE 4
Institutionalize the Program

The least well-defined area of technology staff development is institutionalization. This process involves evaluation of the TLMs. They must be scrutinized for refinement or abandonment. Questions arising from the Technology Adoption Model (TAM) in Chapter 10, such as effectiveness, cost, compatibility, complexity, equity, abandonment, and modification, must be asked by technology staff development committees.

As these decisions are made, public relations becomes a central strategy for institutionalizing TLMs. Public relations about the TLMs include the following:

1. Making presentations to civic and social organizations.

2. Sending memos to major constituencies.

3. Placing notices on bulletin boards—both traditional and electronic.

4. Sending out newsletters.

5. Providing articles, newsletters, updates, status reports, or new directions of the projects.

6. Using cable TV to highlight achievements.

SUMMARY

A well-defined technology staff development program must be in place to support TLMs. The technology staff development program takes considerable thought and can not be implemented without a comprehensive plan. Once in place, the TLMs have the potential to transform the learning process and create learners for the 21st century.

20 Rules for Technology Staff Development Activities

1. Participants must physically take part in activities—hands on.

2. Participants must acquire classroom skills.

3. Participants must receive rewards (money, time, recognition).

4. Participants must be volunteers.

5. Participants must produce something.

6. Participants must include building and district administrators.

7. Activities must have the three parts of the Joyce & Showers model: theory/practice/coaching.

8. Activities must be related to perceived needs.

9. Activities must develop a concept.

10. Activities must include a plan of action.

11. Activities must include an opportunity for follow-up practice.

12. Activities must address creature comforts.

13. Activities must include shared learning with colleagues.

14. Activities must take place in a training facility for adults.

15. Activities must be fun.

16. Activities must take people from where they are.

17. Activities must address multiple intelligences and learning styles.

18. "Hot-line" help is a must.

19. Teachers must work in a "one-plug" or "one switch" environment.

20. The technology must be present in the classroom.

Figure 5

IRI/SkyLight Training and Publishing

CHAPTER 11

Recommended Readings for Chapter 11: Staff Development

Bailey, G. D., and G. Bailey. 1993. *101 activities for creating effective technology staff development programs: A sourcebook of games, stores, role playing and learning exercises for administrators.* New York: Scholastic.

Bailey, G. D., and D. Lumley. 1994. *Technology staff development programs: A leadership sourcebook for administrators.* New York: Scholastic.

Costa, A. 1991. Staff developers: Tinkerers or transformers: Nine perspecitives on the future of staff developement. *Journal of Staff Development,*12(1), 5-6.

Fullan, M. G., and S. Stiegelbauer. 1991. *The new meaning of educational change.* New York: Teacher's College.

Hort, S. M. 1992. *Facilitiative leadership: The imperative for change.* Austin, TX: Southwest Educational Development Laboratory.

Joyce, B., and B. Showers. 1988. *Student achievement through staff development.* New York: Longman.

Marshall, G. 1988. Computer training for teachers must be practical and relevant. *Executive Educator 10*(3): 26–27.

November, A. 1993. Risky business: Redefining professional development. *Electronic Learning 12*(5): 16.

Schlechty, P. C. 1993. On the frontier of school reform with trailblazers, pioneers, and settlers. *Journal of Staff Development 14*(4): 46–51.

Venditti, P. N. 1994. From hermit to helper: A taxonomy of technological experts in education. *Educational Technology 34*(6): 48–50.

PART IV

Resources for Technology Adoption

Glossary

The following definitions may help teachers and technology leaders become familiar with the terms used in restructuring with technology.

Analog: Analog signals are stored as a continuous, smooth wave that mimics the waves of the original (Apple Computer Inc. 1991). Unfortunately the quality of analog signals deteriorate over time. Each time a sound is copied it looses some fidelity and when transmitted picks up extraneous noise (U. S. Congress, Office of Technology Assessment 1988).

Animation: The imitation of movement produced by showing a series of images on the screen (Microsoft 1991).

ASCII (text) files: An ASCII (American Standard for Code Information Interchange) is one which is composed entirely of characters that can by typed from a keyboard. It contains no graphics or special codes for printing (Jordahl 1991). ASCII assigns a numeric value to letters (Microsoft 1991).

Audio teleconferencing: Audio teleconferencing is a distance technology that uses telephones and speakerphones to allow more than one person to speak or listen (Whisler 1988).

Audiographic systems: Audiographic systems use computers as interactive electronic chalkboards and two-way audio conferencing (Whisler 1988).

Backbone: Backbone is a central network that connects several other, usually lower-bandwidth networks or computing devices so they can communicate electronically with each other (Ohlson & Michael 1992).

Backup: A copy of a program, disk, or document to insure the safety of the original against loss (Microsoft 1991).

Bandwidth: Bandwidth is the information carrying capacity of a communications system, generally measured in bps. (Ohlson & Michael 1992).

Battery backup: A battery-operated supply used as an alternative source of power in the event of electrical failure (Microsoft 1991).

Baud/bps: Both baud and bps (bits per second) refer to the rate of speed at which information is transferred via modem over a phone connection (Jordahl 1991).

BBS: The BBS (bulletin board system) is an area within a network where users "post" information for public display (Jordahl 1991).

Bells and whistles: A jargon term used to describe extra features added to hardware or software unneeded to insure basic operation (Microsoft 1991).

Binary Files: Binary files are those containing information not represented in the file by ASCII characters. These may be graphics, formatted files, or even programs (Jordahl 1991).

BITNET: BITNET (Because It's Time NETwork) is the U.S. network linking colleges, universities, and research institutions (Jordahl 1991).

Boolean: This is a type of mathematical expression having to do with true and false values, rather than numerical calculations. Many computer operations rely on the Boolean logical operators of "and," "or," and "not" (Microsoft 1991).

Broadband network: A type of local area network on which transmissions travel as radio-frequencies on separate channels. It can handle significantly higher rates of transmission over greater distances than baseband (Microsoft 1991).

Bus network: A topology for a local area network in which all devices are connected to a main line of communication (Microsoft 1991).

CAD/CAM: Computer-Aided Design/Computer-Aided Manufacturing.

CD-Audio: CD-Audio is sound interactively accessed by a computer from ordinary compact discs such as those on sale in record stores (Apple Computer, Inc. 1991).

CD-I: Compact Disc-Interactive, a hardware and software standard for optical disc technology that combines audio, video, and text on high capacity compact discs (Microsoft 1991).

CD-ROM: Compact Disk-Read Only Memory. A variant of audio compact disk that stores extremely large amounts of data—including text, graphics, animation, sound, and video for future use by a computer (Apple Computer, Inc. 1991). CD-ROM drives are separate from disks. As the discs are relatively cheap with a large storage capacity they are appropriate for distribution of a multimedia course. However they cannot be modified by the user.

Clip art: A collection of photographs, diagrams, maps, drawings, and graphics that can be "clipped" from the collection and incorporated into documents (Microsoft 1991).

Coaxial cable: Coaxial cable is an electrical cable consisting of a wire surrounded by a cylindrical conductor which has the same axis (Ohlson & Michael 1992).

Collaborative learning: Collaborative learning is when a group sets out to discover or create an understanding of a significant phenomenon. Collaboration is a purposive relationship derived to solve a problem or discover something (Schrage 1990).

Cooperative learning: Robert Slavin's (1983) cooperative learning model is based on specific group rewards for team members' learning and task specialization. Cooperative learning asks students to work together to solve problems, locate information, and make presentations (Bruce 1992).

Computer literacy: Knowledge and an understanding of computers combined with the ability to use them effectively (Microsoft 1991).

Conferencing: A term used to indicate when several network users communicate on a particular subject (Jordahl 1991).

Connect time charges: These refer to the fees network information sources charge users for the time they spend online (Jordahl 1991).

Constructivist Psychology: Learners construct and then reconstruct mental models that organize ideas and their interrelationships (Shepard 1991).

CRT: Cathode-Ray Tube, the basis of the television screens and standard microcomputer screens (Microsoft 1991).

Cyberspace: Another term for virtual reality where users are immersed in a computer generated, three-dimensional world (Lantz 1992).

Daisy chain: A set of devices connected one after another along a single line (Microsoft 1991).

Database: Loosely, any aggregation of data; a file consisting of a number of records each of which is constructed of fields of a particular type, together with a collection of operations that facilitate searching, sorting, and combining activities (Microsoft 1991).

DB Connector: Any of several types of cable ends used to connect serial and parallel input and output ports of computer equipment (Microsoft 1991).

Desktop publishing: The use of computers and specialized software to combine text and graphics to create documents ready for publication (Microsoft 1991).

Digital: Digital technologies refers to signals which have been converted into a series of discrete numerical values. In playback, these numeric values are reproduced exactly, without the distortion that inevitably creeps into older analog methods (Lynch, Apple Corp. 1991; U. S. Congress, Office of Technology Assessment 1988).

Digitized Audio: Allows instructors to incorporate unique audio materials into teaching applications. With audio digitization any sounds or music from a tape, record, CD, or "live" recordings can be captured for used in multimedia teaching projects (Apple, Inc. 1991).

Disk: A round, flat piece of flexible plastic (floppy) or inflexible metal (hard disk) coated with a magnetic material used to store information in digital form (Microsoft 1991).

Distance learning: Distance learning is the use of telecommunications devices—such as satellite, television, fiber optics, telephone, or fax machine—to send instructional programming to learners (Rockman and Lillenthal 1992).

Distributed Network: A distributed network is one where computers are placed in the classroom as opposed to a networked computer lab.

DV-I: Digital Video-Interactive, a hardware/software system using compressed of digital video and audio for use in microcomputer applications (Microsoft 1991).

E-mail: Electronic mail is a computer "mail box" where users receive and send personal letters, belong to public forums, and exchange information with other attached users over electronic connections (Eiser 1990).

Ergometrics: The study of people vis-à-vis their working environment (Microsoft 1991).

Ethernet: A local area network using a bus topography providing baseband transmission at 10 megabytes per second (Microsoft 1991).

Ethernet cable: Cable that meets the specifications for the type of cable that can be use on an ethernet network (thick or thin coaxial or twisted pair) (Ohlson & Michael 1992).

FAX: A technology used to send documents over phone lines. Text and graphics are reduced to digital form and transmitted to distant locations (Microsoft 1991). Superficially, facsimile machines appear to be much like copiers where the document is "photographed" in one location and printed in another.

Fiberoptic: Fiberoptic wire carries an electrical signal that has been converted to light signals at high speeds across great distance with little distortion (Lipson 1992). Fiber optic is a "cabling" sometimes referred to as glass. Glass filament conducts pulses converted from electrical signals.

Fileserver: A storage device on a network that is accessible to all users of the network (Microsoft 1991).

File-transfer protocols: The method by which files are transferred to or from a host computer. Protocols usually refer to error-correcting procedures that check for problems during transfer and resend incorrect data (Pettacia 1993).

Floppy disk: A round, flat piece of coated plastic encased in a plastic cover and used to store information (Microsoft 1991). Floppy disks are low-capacity, fast-access magnetic storage. They can be used to store text, sound, or graphics, but their low capacity limits their utility in multimedia applications (Kaplan-Neher 1989).

Flowchart: A chart that shows the path data takes through a program (Microsoft 1991).

Footprint: The surface area a personal computer or peripheral occupies on a desktop (Microsoft 1991).

Freeware: Free computer programs (Microsoft 1991).

Freeze frame video: Freeze frame video is a electronic slide show transmitted by video. An instructor uses a video camera focused on a printer, graphic materials, blackboard, or people to capture an image for transmission over a phone line (Whisler 1988).

Garbage In, Garbage Out (GIGO): A computer jargon referring to the nonthinking nature of a computer and its processes (Microsoft 1991).

Gateway: A device or program connecting two LANs using different protocols. Translating these protocols are devices on these two networks to communicate with each other (Ohlson & Michael 1992).

Gigabyte: 1 billion bytes.

Graphical User Interface (GUI): A display format that allows users to choose commands, start programs, and see lists of files and other options by pointing to pictorial representations (icons) and lists of menu items on the screen (Microsoft 1991).

Groupware: A collective term for software that allows users to collaborate gracefully over time and distance (Johnson 1991).

Guide: Guide© is a commercial software product of Owl Inc., which allows authors to use electronic hypertext.

Handshake: A signal acknowledging that communications can take place, usually involving modems and telecommunications (Microsoft 1991).

Hard disk: Hard disks are mass storage devices having a higher storage capacity than floppy disks and faster access than optical storage systems (Syllabus 1989).

Hayes-compatible: An adjective describing modems that respond to the same set of commands as a modem manufactured by Hayes Microcomputer Products. The *de facto* standard for microcomputer modems (Microsoft 1991).

HDTV: High-Definition Television is any production or delivery mechanism designed to display images in real time with 1000 lines of resolution or more (McKinney 1991).

Hologram: A three-dimensional figure created by holography (Microsoft 1991).

Host computer: The mainframe or other personal computer to which your computer is connecting (Pettacia 1993).

Hub: A device that extends the maximum physical length of a network by clearing and retransmitting signals among network segments (Ohlson & Michael 1992).

HyperCard: HyperCard® is a commercial software product of Claris Corporation which allows authors to use electronic hypertext. It has been described as an electronic stack of index cards (Apple Computer, Inc. 1989; Minnesota State Department of Education 1990a).

Hypermedia: Hypermedia is hypertextual documents containing text, graphics, animation, sound, or motion video.

Hypertext: Hypertext consists of chucks of textual information connected associatively (Jonassen 1989).

Icon: A small graphical user image (GUI) displayed on the screen to represent an object that can be manipulated by the user (Microsoft 1991).

Instruction by satellite: Instruction by satellite usually involves a program from a broadcast studio where student and teacher can hear and respond to each other. Some include computer-assisted instruction components; some do not (Whisler 1988).

Internet: Internet is an electronic mail system connecting governmental institutions, military branches, educational institutions, and commercial companies (Jordahl 1991).

Kermit: A telecommunications protocol used mostly by educational institutions and older mainframes. The slowest of all protocols (Pettacia 1993).

LAN: L(ocal) A(rea) N(etworks) are the smallest of networking topologies, usually covering areas less than two miles (Motorola Codex 1992). They often link computers in one building to nearby buildings (Maddux & Willis 1992). A Local Area Network is a group of connected, intercommunicating computers that share peripheral devices residing within a limited geographic area (Ohlson & Michael 1992).

LCD: L(iquid) C(rystal) D(isplay); a type of display that uses a liquid compound to display data (Microsoft 1991).

LOGOFF: LOGOFF is the sequence of events which occur when the caller disconnects from the host system.

LOGON: LOGON is the sequence of events which occur when the caller connects to the host system.

Links: Links are the relations that connect nodes of information in a program such as Linkway® and HyperCard® (Marchionini 1988).

Linkway: Linkway® is an IBM software package that performs similar functions to Claris HyperCard®.

Mainframe: A high-level, expensive computer designed for intensive computations tasks. Because of their complexity and expense, they are often shared by multiple users (Microsoft 1991).

MIDI: M(usical) I(nstrument) D(igital) I(nterface) is the standard way both professional and amateur musicians connect synthesizers, keyboards, and other musical instrument to computers (Bove & Rhodes 1990).

Modem: The device that connects a computer to a phone line and allows data to be transmitted (Jordahl 1991).

Multimedia: Multimedia programs are applications or utilities that integrate text, sound, graphics, still images, animation, and video for computer-generated presentations (Gill 1992). Sometimes a subset of hypermedia (Microsoft 1991).

Network: A group of computers and peripheral devices, such as printers, that are interconnected so they can communicate with each other (Ohlson & Michael 1992).

Nodes: Nodes are the informational units of hypertext: paragraphs, images, articles, lessons, etc. (Marchionini 1988).

NTSC: N(ational) T(elevision) S(ystem) C(ommittee). The organization that established the standard for television production and broadcast. They set the current 525 scanning line per frame standard (McKinney 1991).

Platform: The basic computer system or an organization. The most common platforms are Apple and IBM (Microsoft 1991).

Plotter: Any device used to draw charts, diagrams, and other graphics similar to the work done by draftsmen (Microsoft 1991).

Power user: A person skilled with computers (Microsoft 1991).

Public-domain software: A program donated for public use by its owner (Microsoft 1991).

RGB: R(ed)-G(reen)-B(lue), a mixing model used with many color monitors (Microsoft 1991).

Ring network: A local area network in which devices are connected in a closed loop or ring as opposed to a bus network (Microsoft 1991).

SCSI: S(mall) C(omputer) S(ystem) I(nterface). This is a parallel cabling scheme for connecting peripheral devices such as CD-ROM and color scanners (Microsoft 1991).

Second-Person: Second-person virtual reality systems use a video camera as an input device. Users see their images on a large video monitor or video project image, which the computer processes to include extra features such as their movements, positions, and number of fingers raised.

Server: A server (or file server) is a microcomputer with a large hard drive. It contains the ILS management system, ILS courseware, and student records. It may also contain third-party software (Mageau 1992).

SIMM: S(ingle) I(n-line) M(emory) M(odule). These are devices used to add memory to computers (Microsoft 1991).

Simulation: Simulation programs try to be classroom electronic substitutes for actual experience.

Spell checker: An application program that checks for misspellings in documents.

Spreadsheet program: An application commonly used for finance-related tasks (Microsoft 1991).

Star network: A network scheme where devices are connected to a central computer in a star-shaped topography as opposed to a bus topography (Microsoft 1991).

Telepublishing: The process of transmitting pages of text and graphics via telecommunications for display on a monitor and reproduction (Mulvey 1991).

Terminal emulation: This refers to the ability of the telecommunications software package to imitate a type of computer the host requires. Common settings are TTY or VT100 (Pettacia 1993).

Thicknet: This cable can support longer distances than thinnet (500 meters) and have up to 100 nodes connected to it (Lipson 1992).

Thinnet. This cable looks similar to television cable and is often used to connect networks within limited distances (185 meters) and limited nodes (35) (Lipson 1992).

Token-ring: A networked ring of devices that passes a special bit pattern, called a token, from node to node, deciding which device can transmit data on the network (Ohlson & Michael 1992).

Total Immersion: Virtual reality systems designed to produce a feeling of complete immersion in the environment, using wide-angle stereoscopic, head-mounted displays, simulated three-dimensional audio, and a remote handheld (or glove) manipulator (Lantz 1992).

Turn-key: Turn-key is a term for an ILS installation where the vendor is responsible for installation of the entire system: hardware, wiring, software, and management.

Twisted-pair: This is the type of cable commonly associated with connecting phone line devices (Lipson 1992).

Two-way interactive television: Two-way interactive television provides for real-time two-way visual contact between the instructor and students and generally incorporates an interactive audio component (Whisler 1988).

Upload/Download: Upload refers to sending information over a network. Download refers to receiving information over a network (Jordahl 1991).

Videodisc: Videodisc is a plastic platter that has digitally encoded information in a wide variety of instructional formats: slides, filmstrips, motion pictures, charts, graphs, data, dual audio, illustrations, microfilm, videotape, and text (Minnesota State Department of Education 1991).

WAN: W(ide) A(rea) N(etworks) is a networking topology with national and even international spans (Motorola Codex 1992). Wide Area Network is a group of computer devices connected over long distance often by telephone lines or satellite transmission (Ohlson & Michael 1992).

Web Learning: Knowledge acquisition can be seen as a series of developing structures which are tested, modified, or replaced in ways which facilitate learning and thinking (Shepard 1991).

Word processor: An application program for manipulating text-based documents; the electronic equivalent of paper, pen, typewriter, eraser, and most likely dictionary and thesaurus (Microsoft 1991).

WORM discs: W(rite) O(nce), R(ead) M(any) is an optical storage medium. Currently, WORM drives' access time is slow, but they can store large amounts of information (Kaplan-Neher, 1989).

Virtual reality: Virtual reality is a highly interactive, computer-based multimedia environment which enables users to participate directly in real-time, three-dimensional environments generated by computers (Helsel 1992, Helsel & Roth 1991).

Xmodem: A most common error-checking protocol for use in MODEM transmissions over phone lines (Pettacia 1993).

Ymodem: An error checking protocal for MODEM transmissions. Ymodem is faster than Xmodem (Pettacia 1993).

Zmodem: The fastest error checking protocol of MODEM transmissions (Pettacia 1993).

Vendors

This appendix contains forty-five vendors that have been selected as representative of a growing field of software and hardware suppliers. There are no more that ten vendors for each of the five learning methods. Because the technology and the vendors of educational technology are changing so rapidly, those wishing to implement technology-based learning methods should pay particular attention to vendor listings in trade magazines such as MacWorld, MacUser, PC World, PC User, *and professional magazines such as* T.H.E. Journal, Electronic Learning, *and* Curriculum Product News. *There are literally thousands of firms providing products for electronic learning methods.*

Teacher Centered Learning with Technology

Apple Computer Inc.
20525 Mariani Ave.
Cupertino, CA 95014
800 776-2333

Beagle Brothers
6215 Ferris Square
San Diego, CA 92121
619 452-5500

EduQuest (IBM)
P. O. Box 2150
Atlanta, GA 30055
800 426-3327

Focus Enhancements
800 W. Cummings Park, Suite
Woburn, MA 01801
800 538-8866

Hewlett-Packard
P. O. Box 58059
Santa Clara, CA 95051
800 752-0900

Microsoft Corporation
1 Microsoft Way
Redmond, WA 98052
800 426-9400

Scholastic Software
730 Broadway
New York, NY 10003
800 541-5513

Texas Instruments, Inc.
5701 Airport Rd.
Temple, TX 76503
800 527-3500

TI-IN
1000 Central Parkway North
San Antonio, TX 78232
800 999-8446

Tom Snyder
80 Coolidge Hill Road
Watertown, MA 02172-2817
800-342-2817

Integrated Learning Systems

Computer Curriculum Corporation
1287 Lawrence State Rd.
Sunnyvale, CA 94088
800 227-8324

Computer Networking Specialists
61 E. Main St., P. O. Box 2075
Walla Walla, WA 99362
800 372-3277

Computer Systems Research
Avon Park South, P. O. Box 45
Avon, CT 06001
800 922-1190

Ideal Learning Systems
8505 Freeport Pkwy. Suite 360
Irving, TX 75063
800 999-3234

Josten's Learning Corporation
6170 Cornerstone Court East
San Diego, CA 92121
800 521-8538

New Century Education
220 Old New Brunswick Road
Melville, NY 11747
800 526-4566

TRO/PLATO
4660 W. 77th Street
Edina, MN 55435
800 869-2000

Waastch Education Systems
5250 South 300 West, Suite 350
Salt Lake City, UT 84107
800 877-2848

WICAT Education
1875 South State St.
Orem, UT 85048
800 759-4228

Electronic Collaborative Learning

Applied Engineering
3210 Beltline Road
Dallas, TX 75234
800 554-6227

Asante Technologies
404 Tasman
Sunnyvale, CA 94089
800 662-9686

A. T. & T. Network Systems
475 South St.
Morristown, NJ 07962
800 344-0223

CC: Mail
2141 Landing's Drive
Mountain View, CA 94043
800 448-2500

CE Software
1801 Industrial Circle, P. O. Box
West Des Moines, IA 50265
800 523-7638

Dove Corporation
1200 N. 23rd. Street
Wilmington, NC 28405
800 849-3297

Global Village Communications
685 E. Middlefield Rd., Bldg. B
Mountain View, CA 94043
800 736-4821

Novell, Inc.
122 E. 1700 Street
Provo, UT 84606
800 453-1267

Farallon Computing
2000 Powell St., Suite 600
Emeryville, CA 94608
510 596-9000

Shiva Corporation
One Cambridge Center
Cambridge, MA 02142
800 458-3550

Hyperlearning

Authorware Inc.
275 Shoreline Drive, Suite 535
Redwood City, CA 94065
800 288-9576

Claris Corporation
5201 Patrick Henry Drive
Santa Clara, CA 95052
408 727-8227

Intellimation Library for the
130 Cremona Drive, P. O. Box
Santa Barbara, CA 93116
800 346-8355

IBM Corporation
P.O. Box 2150
Atlanta, GA
800 426-2468

SuperMac Technology
485 Potreto Ave.
Sunnyvale, CA 94086
800 334-3005

Macromedia
600 Townsend St.
San Francisco, CA 94103
415 442-0200

Voyager Company
1351 Pacific Coast Highway
Santa Monica, CA 90401
800 446-2001

Electronic Learning Simulations

Autodesk
2320 Marinship Way
Sausalito, CA 94965
415 332-2344

Broderbund Software Inc.
500 Redwood Blvd., P. O. Box
Novato, CA 94948
800 521-6263

Knowledge Revolution
15 Brush Place
San Francisco, CA 94103
415 553-8153

MECC
6160 Summit Drive North
Minneapolis, MN 55430
800 685-6322

Sony Corporation of America
MD-3-17 Sony Drive
Park Ridge, NJ 07656
201 930-6177

Teaching Technologies
P. O. Box 3808
San Luis Obispo, Ca 93403-3808
805 541-3100

VPL Research Inc.
656 Bair Island Road, Third
Redwood City, CA 94063
415 361-1710

Wings for Learning
1600 Green Hills Road
P.O. Box 660002
Scotts Valley, CA 95067
800 321-7511

Wolfram Research Inc.
100 Trade Center Drive
Champaign, IL 61820
800 451-5151

Blacklines

This section contains blackline masters for transparencies that correspond to Technology-Based Learning Methods or the Technology Adoption Model. Although they may be used with any part of the handbook, they have been grouped to match specific TLMs. These items may prove useful when making presentations to teachers, parents, and other stakeholders.

TEACHING WITH TECHNOLOGY

Effective Schools and Technology

✳

Technology as an Educational Tool

TEACHING WITH TECHNOLOGY

Some Instructional Strategies:

Computer Drill and Practice

*

Lecture with an LCD Panel

*

Videotape Presentation

*

Interactive TV Lessons

*

Mulitmedia Presentation

TEACHING ABOUT TECHNOLOGY

Some Examples:

Willard Dagget

✳

SCANS Report

✳

Technology Preparation Programs

✳

Technology Education Programs

TEACHING ABOUT TECHNOLOGY

Some Instructional Strategies:

Build an Airplane
Build a Bridge

✳

Statistical Control

✳

Computer-Assisted Design
and Manufacturing

EMPOWERING WITH TECHNOLOGY

Some Examples:

Robert Reich:
Symbolic Analyst

*

Marshall McLuhan:
Symbolic Analyst

*

Seymour Papert:
Technology-Infused Environments

EMPOWERING WITH TECHNOLOGY

Some Learning Strategies:

Anyone, Learning
Anything,
Anytime,
Anywhere

Mastering
Technology-Infused
Environments

Information Literacy

Southwestern Kansas

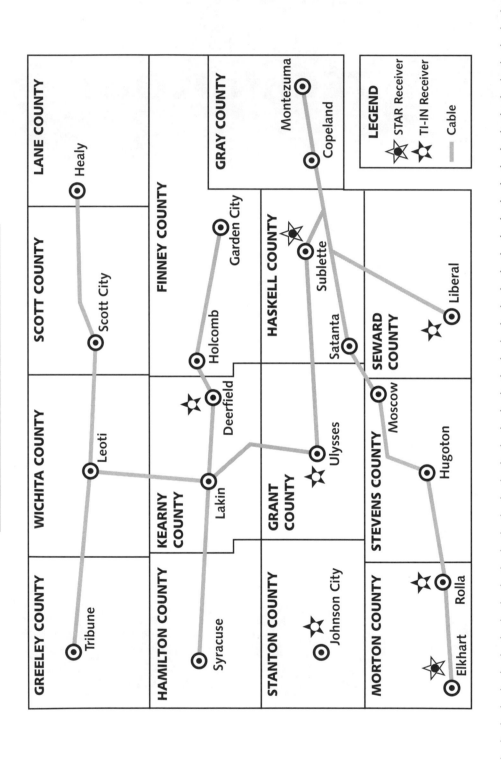

SMART BUYING TACTICS TECHNOLOGY

Performance

*

Cost

*

Expandability

*

Service and Support

*

Design and Construction

IRI/SkyLight Training and Publishing

MAKING YOUR ILS
A SUCCESS

Principal = ILS Leader

✳

Help Teachers Fit ILS into Curriculum

✳

Provide Incentives for Teachers

✳

Give Teachers Time to Preview Lessons

✳

Hire a Competent ILS System Manager

✳

Use the Reports

✳

Have Curriculum-Correlation
Charts Handy

Sample Collaborative Classroom

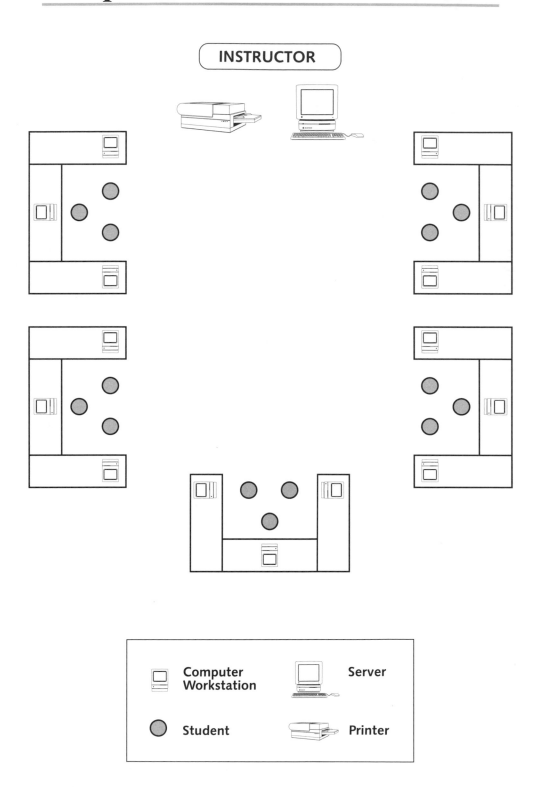

INSTRUCTOR

🖥️ Computer Workstation	🖥️ Server
🔘 Student	🖨️ Printer

Communications Medium and Bandwidth

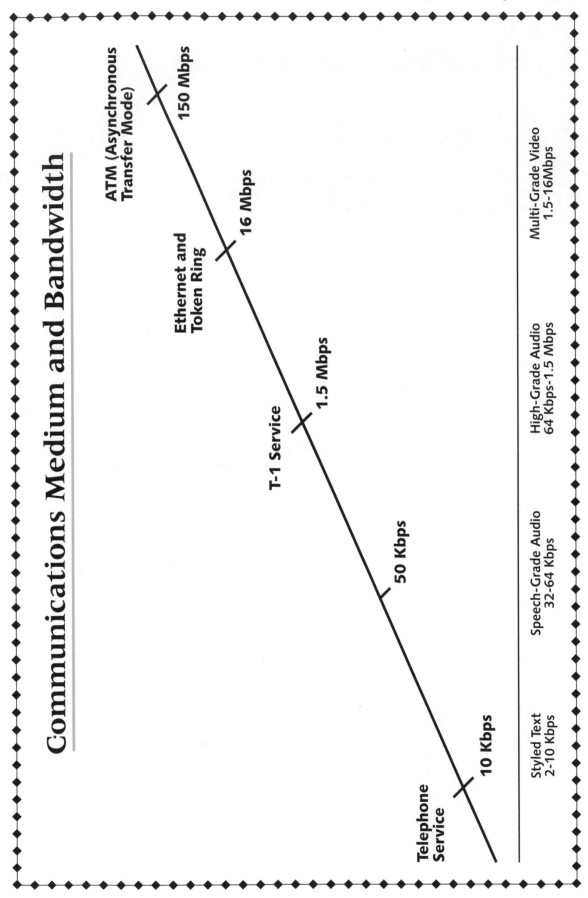

ATM (Asynchronous Transfer Mode) — 150 Mbps

Ethernet and Token Ring — 16 Mbps

1.5 Mbps

T-1 Service

50 Kbps

10 Kbps

Telephone Service

Styled Text
2-10 Kbps

Speech-Grade Audio
32-64 Kbps

High-Grade Audio
64 Kbps-1.5 Mbps

Multi-Grade Video
1.5-16Mbps

Star Topology

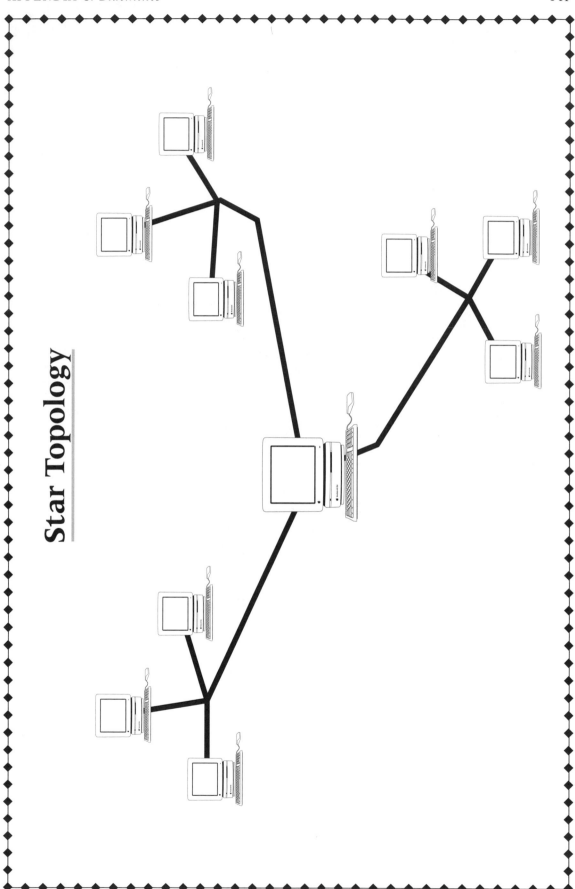

Bus Topology

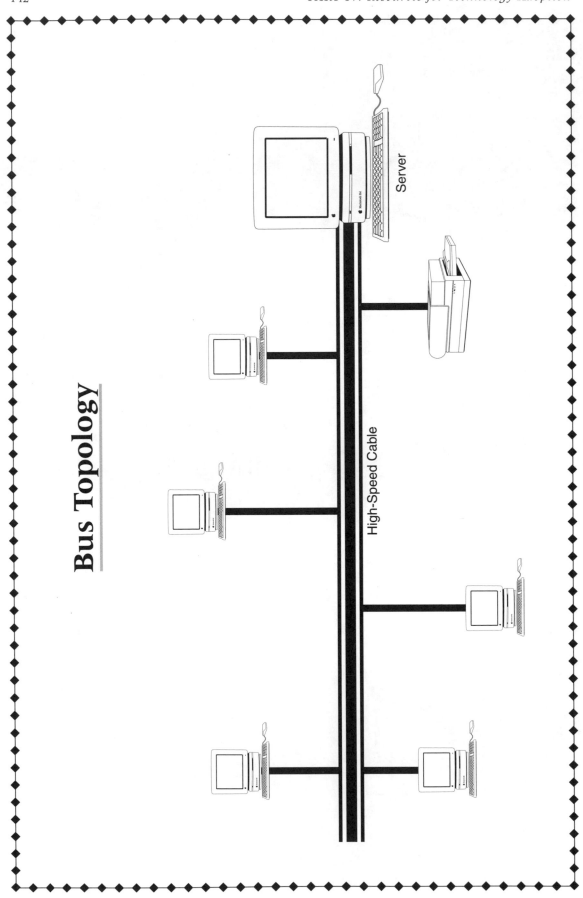

Ring Topology

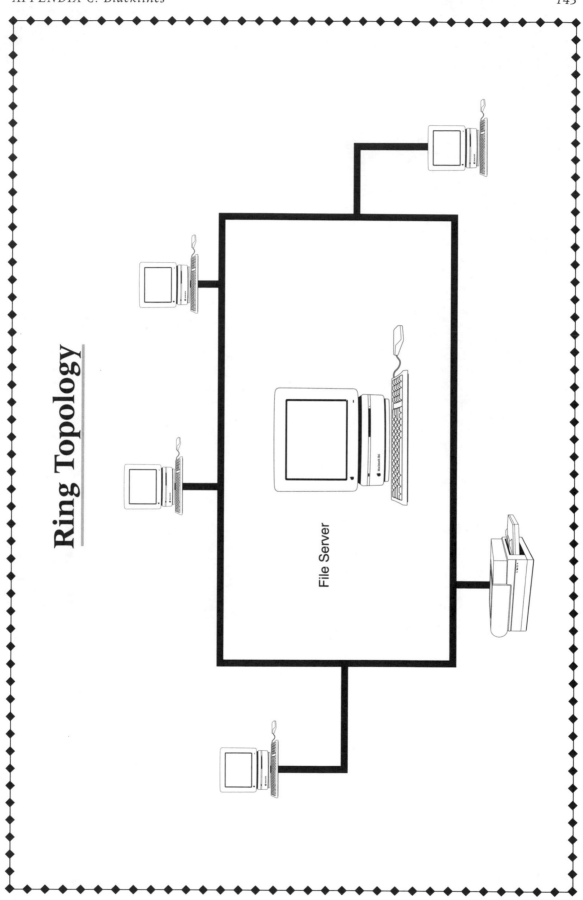

File Server

Checklists

*The following checklists are designed
to help ensure that fundamental issues
have been addressed when implementing
a TLM. The first checklist highlights the
recurring decision elements of the TAM.
The following five checklists are specific
to a chosen TLM in the handbook.
These checklists have been produced in
a size which allows them to be used
as transparencies. The checklists can
be used for discussion with major
stakeholders in the implementation
process and as review for teachers and
principals establishing a TLM.*

Recurring Decision Elements
Technology Adoption Model

_____ **Superiority:** Using this technology provides superior instruction to the students.

_____ **Compatibility:** Software or hardware match with the already installed technology base and curriculum program.

_____ **Cost:** Significant costs have been anticipated. This is a cost-effective way of providing for or improving student learning.

_____ **Complexity:** The equipment or software is within the reach of the people who will be using it.

_____ **Equity:** Equipment and software effectively meet the needs of all student groups: gender, racial, disadvantaged, and socioeconomic.

_____ **Staff Development:** Sufficient technical and development training is provided to insure effectiveness in this chosen method.

_____ **Planned Abandonment:** Plans have been made for abandoning teaching practices which are outdated or replaced by technology-based learning methods.

Teacher-Centered Learning with Technology

_____ **Expandability:** Software or equipment can be expanded and developed to provide greater service to the educational process.

_____ **Curriculum:** Clearly defined curriculum purposes aligned with already installed objectives have been identified.

_____ **Sufficiency:** This technology is complete by itself or part of a larger project.

_____ **Evaluation:** Evaluation of teachers using this technology adequately reflects new teaching styles using emerging technologies.

_____ **Assessment:** Student assessment includes methods for measuring student learning from emerging technology instruction.

_____ **"Hot-Line Help":** Prompt support to solve minor technical difficulties for teachers using technology is available.

_____ **Time:** Time periods for distance learning opportunities have been accommodated.

_____ **Cart:** The cart chosen for teacher use of technological equipment is

- Sturdy
- On large wheels
- Accessible to all classrooms
- "Plug & Play"
- Assigned to an individual for support and scheduling

_____ **Software Selection:** Software selection procedures have been established which insure for teacher and community input.

_____ **Distance Learning:** Staff concerns for distance learning have been addressed. Specifically:

- Certification of teachers
- Negotiated agreements
- Responsibilities of the local district
- Time and place of delivery

_____ **Security:** Procedures for protecting the hardware and software from theft, vandalism, and unauthorized duplications have been established.

_____ **Electricity:** Classrooms have adequate electrical outlets to operate the equipment without unsightly and dangerous extension cords.

_____ **Lighting:** Classroom lighting can be controlled by the teacher for maximum effectiveness of the technology.

Integrated Learning Systems

_____ **Expandability:** Software or equipment can be expanded and developed to provide greater service to the educational process.

_____ **Curriculum:** Clearly defined curriculum purposes aligned with already installed objectives have been identified.

_____ **Curriculum Guides:** Curriculum guides which match the ILS with the classroom curriculum have been prepared for all teachers.

_____ **Training:** Plans for required training of both teachers and lab monitors are in place.

_____ **Licensing Agreements:** Clearly spelled out ownerships, upgrade renewals, and maintenance of the instructional and managerial software are in place.

_____ **Lab v. Classroom Placement:** Placement of the ILS has been decided and planned for, including both room and staff development.

_____ **Facility:** Placement and facility considerations have been addressed for comfort, safety, and security.

_____ **Management and Reporting:** Effective use of the management and reporting capabilities of the ILS has been planned for to include parent communication and student educational programming modification.

_____ **Software Selection:** Software selection procedures have been established which insure for teacher and community input.

Electronic Collaborative Learning

_____ **Collaboration:** Collaborative and cooperative learning models are understood and in place.

_____ **Roles:** Roles are clearly assigned within the collaborative learning model, even though distance and time are involved.

_____ **Literacy:** Information literacy is an applied concept with students and faculty able to electronically search and communicate over time and distance.

_____ **Time:** Different class times and and time zones have been anticipated.

_____ **Security:** Security of the network from a variety of threats has been planned for during the installation phase of an electronic network. These threats include viruses, unauthorized access, and software piracy

_____ **Communicative Compatibility:** Communication devices at all locations are compatible and use the same protocols for effective networking.

_____ **Staff Development:** Staff development for the multiple computer skills required for technology-based cooperative learning has been put in place.

Hyperlearning

_____ **Assessment:** Designs for assessment of student centered learning are in place and clearly communicated to students, parents, and teachers.

_____ **Cognitive Overload:** Attention to the dangers of "swamping" students in a sea of knowledge has been addressed.

_____ **Search Strategies:** Students have acquired adequate search strategies and tactics for the level of student-centered learning expected.

_____ **Navigation:** Students becoming lost in Hyperlearning environments is a real possibility. Navigation standards have been established at the beginning. Plans for a balance between control and unbridled wandering have been established.

_____ **Web & Constructionist Theories of Learning:** Staff development for these theories of learning is in place.

Electronic Learning Simulation

_____ **Gaming:** Safeguards have been installed to insure the simulation matches the curriculum and students do not play "games" with little educational merit.

_____ **Assessment:** Student assessment is addressed in the chosen electronic learning simulation.

_____ **Future:** As simulation is a rapidly expanding field of electronic technology, a view to the future of learning simulations (Virtual Reality) is maintained.

_____ **Ethics:** Ethical considerations of multi-sensory instruction is anticipated and supervised.

_____ **Software Selection:** Software selection procedures have been established which insure for teacher and community input.

Bibliography

The following books and articles have been used in the construction of this handbook. Readers are strongly encouraged to explore many of the different references listed.

Abramson, G. W. 1993. LinkWay features and design. *The Computing Teacher 21*(2): 16–21.

Ackerman, E. 1995. *Learning to use the Internet*. Wilsonville, OR: Franklin Beedle & Associates.

Adams, D. M., and M. Hamm. 1987. *Electronic learning: Issues and teaching ideas for educational computing, television and visual literacy.* Springfield, IL: Charles C. Thomas.

Ambrose, D. W. 1991. The effects of hypermedia on learning: A literature review. *Educational Technology 31*(6): 51–55.

Anderson-Inman, L. 1994. Literacy instruction in an integrated curriculum. *The Computing Teacher 21*(4): 33–36.

Apple Computer, Inc. 1990. *Multimedia in education: Tools for the way people learn.* Cupertino, CA: Apple Computer Inc.

———. 1991. *Teaching, learning & technology—A planning guide.* Cupertino, CA: Apple Computer Inc.

Armstrong, T. 1993. *Seven kinds of smart: Identifying and developing your many intelligences.* New York: Penguin Books.

Bailey, G. D., ed. 1993. *Computer-based intergrated learning systems.* Englewood Cliffs, NJ: Educational Technology Publications.

Bailey, G. D., and G. Bailey. 1993. *101 activities for creating effective technology staff development programs: A sourcebook of games, stores, role playing and learning exercises for administrators.* New York: Scholastic.

Bailey, G. D., and D. Lumley. 1994. *Technology staff development programs: A leadership sourcebook for administrators.* New York: Scholastic.

Barker, J. A. 1992. *Future edge: Discovering the new paradigms of success.* New York: William Morrow and Co.

Bassett, E. 1992. New technology for video conferences. *Electronic Learning 11*(8): 20.

Bauer, D. G. 1993. *The principal's guide to grant success.* New York: Scholastic.

Becker, H. J. 1992. A model for improving performance of integrated learning systems: Mixed individualized/groups/whole class lessons, cooperative learning, and organizing time for teacher led remediation of small groups. *Educational Technology 32*(9): 6–15.

Bell, T. H., and D. L. Elmquist. 1992. Technology: A catalyst for restructuring schools. *Electronic Learning 11*(5): 10–11.

Bevilacqua, A. F. 1989. *Hypertext: Behind the hype.* (ERIC Document Reproduction Service No. 308 882.)

Bittinger, A. 1991, June 11. Video network to connect students in 7 schools. *Salina Journal* 1, 7.

Bixler, B., and J. Spotts. 1994. SCORE courseware offers model for adult learners. *T.H.E. Journal 21*(11): 76–79.

Boudrot, T. E., and C. A. Haugsness. 1988. *Planning for computer instruction and educational technology: From district plans to building implementation.* Topeka, KS: Kansas State Department of Education.

Bove, T., and C. Rhodes. 1990. *Que's macintosh multimedia handbook.* Carmel, IN.

Bracey, G. W. 1988. The impact of computers. *Phi Delta Kappan 70*(1): 70–74.

———. 1991. ILS research isn't helpful. *Electronic Learning 11*(1): 16.

———. 1992a. The bright future of integrated learning systems. *Educational Technology 32*(9): 60–62.

———. 1992b. Computers and cooperative learning. *Electronic Learning 11*(5): 14.

———. 1992c. Creative writing: Do word processors help or hurt student's creativity? *Electronic Learning 12*(3): 12.

———. 1993. Assessing the new assessments. *Principal 72*(3): 34–36.

Branscum, D. 1992. Budget computing. *MacWorld 9*(11): 59–62.

Brewer, T. 1991. 10 Teacher tips for using multimedia. *Electronic Learning 10*(4): 14.

Bruce, C. 1992. Chip Bruce's taxonomy of educational technology applications. *The Holmes Group Forum 6*(2): 10.

Bruder, I. 1989a. Distance learning: What's holding back this boundless delivery system? *Electronic Learning 8*(6): 30–35.

———. 1989b. Future teachers: Are they prepared? *Electronic Learning 8*(4): 32–39.

———. 1989c. New ideas for professional development. *Electronic Learning 9*(3): 22–28.

———. 1990. Restructuring through technology. Special Supplement to *Business week No. 3191:* 32–38.

———. 1991. Distance learning. *Electronic Learning 11*(3): 20–28.

———. 1992a. Can technology help? *Electronic Learning 12*(3): 18–19.

———. 1992b. What's new in NETWORKS? *Electronic Learning 12*(3): 14.

———. 1992c. What's new in MULTIMEDIA? *Electronic Learning 12*(1): 16.

———. 1992d. QUANTUM Leap. *Electronic Learning 12*(1): 22.

———. 1993. Alternative assessment: Putting technology to the test. *Electronic Learning 12*(4): 22–29.

Bruder, I., H. Buchsbaum, M. Hill, and L. C. Orlando. 1992. School reform: Why you need technology to get there. *Electronic Learning 11*(8): 22–28.

Buerry, K., B. Haslan, and D. Legters. 1990. Images of potential: From vision to reality. Special Reprint from *Business Week No. 3191:* 50–53.

Burry, K. 1993. The earth day treasure hunt: Using online resources as a research tools. *The Computing Teacher 21*(1): 53–54.

Bush, V. 1945. The way we may think. *The Atlantic 176*(1): 101–8.

Butzin, S. M. 1992. Project CHILD: A new twist on integrated learning systems. *T. H. E. Journal 20(2)*: 90–94.

Cawelti, G. 1991. Clarifying the means and ends of restructuring. *Update: ASCD 33*(8): 2.

Center for Children and Technology: Bank Street College. 1990. *Application in educational assessment: Future technologies.* (ERIC Document Reproduction Service No. 340 773.)

Center for Learning Technologies. 1984. *Getting started: Planning and implementing computer instruction in schools.* Albany, NY: Center for Learning Technologies.

Cetron, M., and M. Gayle. 1991. *Educational renaissance: Our schools at the turn of the twenty-first century.* New York: St. Martin's Press.

Collins, A. 1991a. Cognitive apprenticeship and instructional technology. In *Educational values and cognitive instruction: Implications for reform,* edited L. Idon and B. F. Jones. Hillsdale NJ: Lawrence Erlbaum Associates.

———. 1991b. The role of computer technology in restructuring schools. *Phi Delta Kappan 73*(1): 28–36.

Collis, B. 1988. *Computers, curriculum, and whole-class instruction.* Belmont, CA: Wadsworth.

Comer, D. E. 1995. *The internet.* Englewood Cliffs, NJ: Prentice Hall.

Cringely, R. X. 1992. Welcome to the future. *Success 39(7)*: 22–28.

Cuban, L. 1988. *The managerial imperative: The practice of leadership in schools.* Albany, NY: State University of New York Press.

———. 1992. Computers meet classroom: Classroom wins. *Education Week 12*(10): 36–37.

Daggett, W. R. 1989. The changing nature of work—A challenge to education. Speech to Kansas Legislators.

Daiute, C. 1992. Multimedia computer: Extending the resource of kindergarten to writers across the grades. *Language Arts 69*(4): 250–60.

David, J. L. 1989. Synthesis of research on school-based management. *Educational Leadership 46*(8): 45–53.

———. 1991. Restructuring with technology. *Phi Delta Kappan 73(1)*: 28–36.

Dede, C. 1987. Empowering environments, hypermedia and microworlds. *The Computing Teacher 15*(3): 20–24.

———. 1988. The role of hypertext in transforming information into knowledge. NECC Conference, Dallas, TX.

———. 1989a. The evolution of information technology: Implications for curriculum. *Educational Leadership 47*(1): 23–26.

———. 1989b. Planning guidelines for emerging instructional technologies. *Educational Technology 29*(4): 7–12.

———. 1992. Making the most of multimedia. "The electronic school," supplement to the *American School Board Journal 178(*9): A13–A15.

Delaney, B. 1994. Virtual reality lands the job. *New Media 4*(8): 40–48.

Deming, W. E. 1986. *Out of the crisis.* Cambridge, MA: Massachusetts Institute of Technology.

Dervarics, C. 1991a. Learning systems even the odds. *Executive Educator, 13(*10), Special supplement, "The electronic school: Innovative uses of technology in education," A21–A22.

———. 1991b. Technology speeds school restructuring. *Executive Educator, 13*(10), Special supplement, "The electronic school: Innovative uses of technology in education," A19–A21.

Dickinson, D. 1992. Multiple technologies for multiple intelligences. "The electronic school," supplement to the *American School Board Journal 178*(9): A8–A12.

D'Ignazio, F. 1988. Bringing the 1990s to the classroom of today. *Phi Delta Kappan 71*(4): 25–31.

———. 1989a. Multimedia on wheels. *The Computing Teacher 17(*2): 24–27.

———. 1989b. Welcome to the multimedia sandbox. *The Computing Teacher 19(*3): 27–28.

———. 1989–90. Through the looking glass: The multiple layers of multimedia. *The Computing Teacher 17*(4): 25–31.

———. 1990a. An inquiry centered classroom of the future. *The Computing Teacher 17*(6): 16–19.

———. 1990b. Electronic highways and the classroom of the future. *The Computing Teacher 17*(8): 20–24.

———. 1990c. Multimedia copyright. *The Computing Teacher 17*(5): 32–35.

———. 1990d. Multimedia horsepower: How much is enough? *The Computing Teacher 17*(7): 16–18.

———. 1990e. Multimedia training centers: The highest tech at affordable prices. *The Computing Teacher 18(*2): 54–55.

———. 1991a. Scavenged inquiry centers: Multimedia learning on wheels. Packet from author.

———. 1991b. Integrating the work environment of the 1990s into today's classrooms. *T.H.E. Journal 18*(11): 95.

———. 1991c. A new curriculum paradigm: The fusion of technology, the arts, and classroom instruction. *The Computing Teacher 18(*2): 54.

———. 1992a. Getting a jump on the future. *Electronic Learning 12(*3): 28–31.

————. 1992b. Toward a collaborative environment. *T.H.E. Journal,* Special Multimedia Supplement, 34.

————. 1992c. Restructuring knowledge: Opportunities for classroom learning in the 1990s. *The Computing Teacher 18*(1): 22–25.

Droegemueller, L. 1991. *Distance learning: A plan for telecommunications in Kansas.* Topeka, KS: Kansas State Department of Education.

Economist. 1991. Television in schools: Pupils or consumers? Channel one offers current affairs and advertisements aimed at high school students. *Economist 319 (7705):* 31.

Edwards, L. D. 1994. Educational technology research section: Mathematical explorations in LOGO: Report of a pilot student from Costa Rica. *Educational Technology 34*(5): 56–60.

Eiser, L. 1990. A guide to telecommunication services. *Technology & Learning 11*(3): 36–43.

Electronic Learning. 1991. Integrated Learning Systems: How to buy an ILS. *Electronic Learning,* Special supplement.

————. 1992a. ILS vendors embrace the MAC, *Electronic Learning 11*(6): Special Edition.

————. 1992b. The most complete guide ever to telecommunications. *Electronic Learning 11*(6): 18–27.

————. 1993. Networks: Learning beyond the classroom. *Electronic Learning 12*(7), Special Edition: 6.

English, W. E., and J.C. Hill. 1990. *Restructuring: The principal and curriculum change.* Reston, VA: National Association of Secondary School Principals.

Engst, A. C. 1994. *Internet starter kit.* Indianapolis, IN: Hayden Books.

Farley, C. J. 1991, September 18. Virtual reality is computer's flying carpet. *USA Today,* 1D and 2D.

Finkel, L. 1990. Moving your district toward technology: It's a bit easier now that we know many of the don'ts! *School Administrator* Special issue: 35–37.

————. 1992a. Are ILSes worth the $$? *Electronic Learning 12*(1): 18.

————. 1992b. What does a curriculum director do with technology? *Electronic Learning 11*(8): 16.

Fullan, M. G., and S. Stigelbauer. 1991. *The new meaning of educational change,* 2nd ed. New York: Teachers College Press.

Gardner, H. 1983. *Frames of mind: The theory of multiple intelligences.* New York: Basic Books.

————. 1988. Mobilizing resources for individual-centered learning. In *Technology in education: Looking toward 2020,* edited by R. S. Nickerson and P. Zodhiates. Hillsdale, NJ: Lawrence Erlbaum Associates.

Gathany, N. C., and J. K. Stehr-Green. 1994. Putting life into computer-based training: The creation of an epid-mioglogic case study. *Educational Technology 34*(6): 44–47.

Gibbon, S. Y., Jr. 1987. Learning and instruction in the information age. In *What curriculum for the information age?*, edited by M. A. White. Hillsdale, NJ: Lawrence Erlbaum.

Gill, E. K. 1992. High voltage PCs. *Presentations 6*(9): 25–30.

Goldberg, C. J. 1992. LCD Panels team with projectors. *MacWeek 6*(21): 27–30.

Goodlad, J. L. 1984. *A place called school: Prospects for the future*. New York: McGraw-Hill.

Gore, A. 1990. The digitization of schools. Special reprint from *Business Week No. 3191*: 28–30.

————. 1991, January–February. Information superhighways: The next information revolution. *Futurist*: 21–23.

Graumann, P. 1994. GALAXY classroom: Television for tomorrow. *Technology & Learning 14*(7): 34–38.

Grunwald, P. 1991. Telecommunications in the classroom. Special supplement to *The Executive Educator 13*(10): A4–A11.

Handy, C. 1990. *The age of unreason*. Boston: Harvard Business School Papers.

Hargadon, T. 1992. Communications medium. *New Media 2*(11): 29.

Harris, J. 1994. People-to-people: Projects on the Internet. *The Computing Teacher 21*(4): 48–52.

Helsel, S. K. 1990. *Interactive optical technologies in education and training*. Westport, CT: Meckler.

————. 1992. Virtual reality as a learning medium. *Instructional Delivery Systems 6(*4): 4–5.

Helsel, S. K., and J. P. Roth, eds. 1991. *Virtual reality: Theory, practice and promise*. Westport, CT: Meckler.

Henderson, J. 1991. Designing realities: Interactive media, virtual realities and cyberspace. In *Virtual reality: Theory, practice and promise,* edited by S. K. Helsel and J. P. Roth. Westport, CT: Meckler.

Hertzke, E. R. 1992. The administrator's role in adopting and using Integrated Learning Systems. *Educational Technology 32*(9): 44–45.

Higgins, J. 1990. Electronic schools and American competitiveness. Special reprint from *Business Week No. 3191*: 8–10.

Hill, M. 1992a. The new literacy. *Electronic Learning 12*(1): 28–33.

————. 1992b. What's new in VIRTUAL REALITY. *Electronic Learning 12*(2): 10.

————. 1992c. Writing to learning: Processing writing moves into the curriculum. *Electronic Learning 12*(3): 20–27.

————. 1993a. Blackboard-disk jockeys. *Electronic Learning* Special Edition: 16–17.

————. 1993b. What's new in ILSes? *Electronic Learning 12*(4): 12.

Hodgkinson, H. 1991a. Reform versus reality. *Phi Delta Kappan 73*(1): 9–17.

————. 1991b. Today's curriculum: How appropriate will it be in the year 2000? *NASSP Bulletin* 75(535): 2–7.

Holzberg, C. S. 1994. Technology in special education. *Technology & Learning* 14(7): 18–21.

Hooper, S., and M. J. Hannafin. 1991. Psychological perspectives on emerging instructional technologies: A critical analysis. *Educational Psychologist* 26(1): 69–95.

Hughes, L. 1992. Gaining fluency. *Educational Computing & Technology* 13(8): 33–4.

Hutchins, C. 1993. Lights cameras . . . students. *Electronic Learning* 13(2): 30.

Jacobson, P. 1992. Save the cities! *SimCity* in Grade 2–5. *The Computing Teacher* 20(2): 14–15.

Jancich, H. S. 1991. The evolution of a revolution: Technology in the classroom. *The Balance Sheet* 73(1): 19–21.

Johnson, D. W., and R. T. Johnson. 1985. Cooperative learning: One key to computer assisted learning. *The Computing Teacher* 13(1): 11–13.

————. 1991. *Learning together and alone: Cooperative, competitive and individualistic learning.* Englewood Cliffs, NJ: Prentice Hall.

Johnson, R. 1991. *Leading business teams: How teams can use technology and group process tools to enhance performance.* Reading, MA: Addison-Wesley.

Johnston, J. 1985. Information literacy: Academic skills for a new age. *National Institute of Education, September, 1985*: 3–18.

Jonassen, D. H. 1986. Hypertext principles for text and courseware design. *Educational Psychologist* 21(4): 269–292.

————. 1989. *Hypertext/hypermedia.* Englewood Cliffs, NJ: Educational Technology Publications.

————. 1991. Thinking technology: Context is everything. *Educational Technology* 31(6): 35–37.

————. 1992. Learning vs. information. *Journal of Educational Multimedia and Hypermedia* 1(1): 3–5.

Jordahl, G. 1991. Breaking down classroom walls: Distance learning comes of age. *Technology & Learning* 11(5): 72–78.

Kansas State Department of Education. 1989. *Kansas schools for the 21st Century.* Topeka, KS.

Kaplan-Neher, A. 1989. New media: Dymystifying the technology. *Syllabus No.* 7: 2–8.

Kay, A. C. 1991. Computers, networks and education. *Scientific American* 265(3): 138–48.

Knirk, F. G. 1992. Facility requirements for integrated learning systems. *Educational Technology* 32(9): 26–32.

Koeppel, D. L. 1991. Why channel one may be here to stay. *Marketing Week* 32(23): 22–23.

Komoski, K. 1990. Integrated learning systems take integrated efforts. *School Administrator* Special Issue: 25–27.

Kuhn, T. S. 1962. *The structure of scientific revolutions.* Chicago: University of Chicago Press.

Lantz, E. 1992. Virtual reality in science museums. *Instructional Delivery Systems* 6(4): 10–12.

Leslie, J. 1993. Kids connecting. *Wired* 1(5): 90–93.

Lezotte, L. W. 1989. School improvement based on effective schools research. In *Beyond separate education: Quality education for all,* edited by D. K. Lispky and A. Gartner. Baltimore: P. H. Brookes.

———. 1991. School improvement based on effective schools research: The decade ahead. *Educational Considerations* 18(2): 19–21.

Lindroth, L. K. 1994. Lights, action, math. *Electronic Learning* 13(7): 42–43.

Lipson, S. B. 1992. 10 Base T-hubs: Stars on the ethernet horizon. *MacUser* 8(10): 25–40.

Lumley, D., and G. D. Bailey. 1990. Integrated learning systems: A new method of delivering effective instruction. *Kansas Journal of Educational Technology* 1(1): 5–6.

———. 1993. *Planning for technology: A guidebook for school administrators.* New York: Scholastic.

Maddux, C. D., and J. W. Willis. 1992. Integrated learning systems and their alternatives: Problems and cautions. *Educational Technology* 32(9): 51–57.

Mageau, T. 1990. ILS: Its new role in schools. *Electronic Learning* 10(1): 22–32.

———. 1991. Redefining the textbook. *Electronic Learning* 10(5): 14–18.

———. 1992. Integrating an ILS: Two teaching models that work. *Electronic Learning* 11(4): 16–22.

Male, M. 1986. Cooperative learning for effective mainstreaming. *The Computing Teacher* 14(1): 35–37.

Marchionini, G. 1988. Hypermedia and learning: Freedom and chaos. *Educational Technology* 28(11): 8–12.

Marshall, G. 1990. Drill won't do. *American School Board Journal* 177(7): 21–23.

McCarthy, M. J. 1991. *Mastering the information age: A course in working smarter, thinking better, and learning faster.* Los Angeles, CA: Jeremy P. Tarcher.

McCarthy, R. 1992. Hands on math and science. *Electronic Learning* 12(1): 9–13.

McCarthy, R., and M. Revenaugh. 1989. For basic skills instruction: Integrated learning systems represent a package that won't bite. *Electronic Learning* Special supplement: 13–17.

McCarty, P. 1991. Bringing the world into the classroom. *Principal* 71(2): 8–10.

McKinney, B. C. 1991. The virtual world of HDTV. In *Virtual reality: Theory, practice and promise,* edited by S. K. Helsel and J. P. Roth. Westport, CT: Meckler.

McLellan, H. 1991. Virtual environments and situated learning. *Multimedia Review, Fall:* 30–37.

McLuhan, M. 1962. *The Gutenberg galaxy: The making of typographic man.* Toronto: University of Toronto Press.

McREL. 1990. *National education goals: Can they lead to real reform?* Aurora, CO: McREL.

————. 1992a. Having computers is step one: New schools need to reach out to telecommunications networks. *Research Roundup* November: 3.

————. 1992b. Technologies help teachers overcome time, space barriers and make communication easier. *Research Roundup* November: 1.

Mecklenberger, J. A. 1990. The new revolution. Special reprint *Business week No. 3191:* 22–26.

Meeks, B. 1991. Computers for communication. In *Computers, cognition and development,* edited by J. Rutkowska and C. Crook. Los Angeles, CA: Jeremy P. Tarcher.

Microsoft Press. 1991. *Computer dictionary.* Redmond, WA: Microsoft Press.

Miles, S. 1991. Project 2000: Surrattsville High School Model Telecommunications and School Restructuring: An interactive videoconference presented by the National School Board Association, October 31, 1991.

Mill, H. 1988. *An administrator's manual for the use of microcomputers in the schools.* Englewood Cliffs, NJ: Prentice-Hall.

Minnesota Department of Education. 1990a. *Desktop multimedia in the classroom.* St. Paul, MN: Minnesota Department of Education.

————. 1990b. *Hypermedia in the classroom.* St. Paul, MN: Minnesota Department of Education (videotape).

Mojkowski, C. 1990. 10 Essential truths to help you plan for technology use. *Tech Trends, 30*(7): 18–22.

Molnar, A. R. 1990. Computers in education: A historical perspective of the unfinished task. *T.H.E. Journal 18*(4): 80–83.

Morehouse, D. E., and S. H. Stockdill. 1992. Technology adoption model. *Educational Technology 32(2):* 57–59.

Morehouse, D. L., M. L. Hoaglund, and R. H. Schmidt. 1987. Interactive television findings, issues and recommendations: An analysis based on evaluation of Minnesota's Technology Demonstration Program. Unpublished, Feb. 1, 1987.

Morse, R. H. 1991. Computer uses in secondary science education. *ERIC Digest EDO-1R-91-1:* 1–2.

Motorola Codex. 1992. *The basics book of information networking.* Reading, MA: Addison-Wesley.

Muller, D. G., and R. Leonetti. 1992. A major technological advancement in training. *Instructional Delivery Systems 6(4):* 15–17.

Mulvey, W. 1991. The dynamics of telepublishing, telecommunications and school restructuring: An interactive videoconference presented by the National School Board Association, October 31, 1991.

Nadler, G., and S. Hibino. 1990. *Breakthrough thinking: Why we must change the way we solve problems and the seven principles to achieve this.* Rocklin, CA: Prima Publishing.

Naisbitt, J., and P. Aburdene. 1990. *Megatrends 2000: Ten new directions for the 1990s.* New York: Avon Books.

National Commission on Excellence in Education. 1983. *A nation at risk: The imperative for educational reform*, Washington, DC: U.S. Government Printing Office.

National Education Goals Panel. 1991. *The national educational goals report: Building a nation of learners.* Washington, DC: National Education Goals Panel.

National School Boards Association. 1995. *Plans & policies for technology in education.* Alexandria, VA: National School Boards Association.

NCSA Applications. 1994. *Virtual Back Hoe.* Mosaic address http://www.ncsa.uiuc.edu. VR/VR/vr_pp_ct.

Nelson, T. 1987. *Computer lib/dream machines.* Redmond, WA: Tempus Books.

Newhard, R. 1987. Converting information into knowledge: The promise of CD-ROM. *Wilson Library Bulletin 62*(4): 36–38.

Newman, D. 1992. Technology as support for school structure and school restructuring. *Phi Delta Kappan 74*(4): 308–315.

Newman, F. M. 1991. Linking restructuring to authentic student achievement. *Phi Delta Kappan 72*(6): 458–463.

Nix, D. 1990. Should computers know what you can do with them? In *Cognition, education and multimedia: Exploring ideas in high technology*, edited by D. Nix and R. J. Spiro. Hillsdale, NJ: Lawrence Erlbaum Associates.

Nix, D., and R. Spiro, eds. 1990. *Cognition, educational multimedia: Exploring ideas in high technology.* Hillsdale, NJ: Lawrence Erlbaum Associates.

Novelli, J. 1993. Better tools for better teamwork. *Instructor 103*(3): 43–45.

November, A. 1992a. Brave new world revisited? *Electronic Learning 11*(6): 50.

———. 1992b. Familyware. *Electronic Learning 11*(7): 50.

———. 1992c. Enabling teachers to become researchers. *Electronic Learning 11*(8): 58.

———. 1992d. The promised land: Looking to Moses for a lesson on restructuring. *Electronic Learning 12*(1): 20.

Office of Technology Assessment. 1995. *Teachers & technology: Making the connection.* Washington, D. C.: U.S. Government Printing Office.

Ohlson, K. J., and A. Michael. 1992. LocalTalking in LAN land: A glossary. *MacUser 8*(10): 45–50.

Olson, G., and D. E. Atkins. 1990. Supporting collaboration with advances in multimedia electronic mail: The NSF EXPRESS project. In *Intellectual teamwork: Social and technological foundation of cooperative work,* edited by J. Galegher, R. E. Kraut, and C. Egido. Hillsdale, NJ: Lawrence Erlbaum Associates.

Papert, S. 1980. *Mindstorms: Children, computers, and powerful ideas.* New York: Basic Books, Inc.

———. 1984. New theories for new learnings. *School Psychology Review 13*(4): 422–28.

———. 1993. *The children's machine: Rethinking school in the age of the computer.* New York: Basic Books.

Papert, S., and I. Herel, eds. 1990. *Constructionism.* Norwood, NJ: Albex.

Pea, R. D. 1984. Beyond amplification: Using the computer to reorganize mental functioning. *Education Psychologist 13*(4): 168–82.

Pearlman, R. 1989. Technology's role in restructuring schools. *Electronic Learning 8*(8): 8–14.

———. 1991. Restructuring with technology: A tour of schools where it's happening. *Technology & Learning 11*(4): 30–37.

Perelman, L. J. 1988. Restructuring the system is the solution. *Phi Delta Kappan 70*(1): 20–24.

———. 1990a. Change equals choice plus technology: Without both, schools are headed for history's scrapheap. *Teacher Magazine October:* 59–60.

———. 1990b. A new learning enterprise. *Business Week No. 3191,* Special Supplement: 10–20.

———. 1992. *School's out: Hyperlearning, the new technology, and the end of education.* New York: William Morrow and Company.

Pettacia, T. 1993. Making connections. *MacUser 9*(2): 100–106.

Pritchard, W. H., and J. D. Busby. 1991. A blueprint for successfully integrating technology into your institution, *T.H.E. Journal,* Macintosh Special Issue: 48–52.

Privateer, P. M., and C. MacCrate. 1992. Odyssey project: A search for new learning solutions. *T.H.E. Journal 20*(3): 76–80.

Provenzo, E. F., Jr. 1986. *Beyond the Gutenberg galaxy: Microcomputers and the emergence of the post-typographic culture.* New York: Teachers College Press.

Ravitch, D. 1987. Technology and the curriculum: Promise and peril. In *What curriculum for the information age?,* edited by M. A. White. Hillsdale, NJ: Lawrence Erlbaum Associates.

Ray, D. 1989. Administrators have a crucial role to play in transforming education. *Electronic Learning 8*(4): 6–8.

———. 1992. Educational technology leadership for the age of restructuring. *The Computing Teacher 9*(6): 8–14.

Reich, R. B. 1991. *The work of nations: Preparing ourselves for 21st century capitalism.* New York: Alfred A. Knopf.

Reissman, R. 1992. A biosphere research expedition. *The Computing Teacher 20*(1): 30–32.

Reveaux, T. 1992. Virtual reality gets real. *New Media 3*(1): 32–33.

Rezabek, R. A. 1989. *Elaborated resources: An instructional design strategy for hypermedia.* (ERIC Document Reproduction Service No. 316 175.)

Rist, M. 1991. Whittling away at public education. *The Executive Educator 13*(9): 22–28.

Rockman, S., and K. Lillenthal. 1992. Today's distance learning. *Inventing Tomorrow's Schools 2*(1): 5–6.

Ross, T. W. 1992. A principal's guide to ILS facilities installation. *Educational Technology 32*(9): 33–35.

Ruthven, K. 1985. Theory into practice. In *Information technology in education: Signposts and research directions*, edited by D. J. Smith. London: Economics and Social Research Council.

Sarason, S. B. 1990. *The predictable failure of educational reform: Can we change course before it's too late?* San Francisco: Jossey-Bass Publishers.

Schneiner, B. 1993. Data guardians: How strong are the software locks on 24 security products? *MacWorld 19*(2): 145–51.

Schrage, M. 1990. *Shared minds: The new technologies of collaboration.* New York: Random House.

Schwartz, J. L. 1987. Closing the gap between education and schools. In *What curriculum for the information age?*, edited by M. A. White. Hillsdale, NJ: Lawrence Erlbaum Associates.

Secretary's Commission on Achieving Necessary Skills, U.S. Department of Labor. 1991. *What work requires of schools.* Washington, DC: U.S. Government Printing Office.

Senge, P. M. 1990. *The fifth discipline: The art & practice of the learning organization.* New York: Doubleday.

Sergiovanni, T. J. 1989. Value driven schools. In *Organzing for learning: Towards the 21st Century,* edited by J. J. Walberg and J. J. Lane. Reston, VA: National Association of Secondary School Principals.

Sheingold, K. 1991. Restructuring for learning with technology: The potential for synergy. *Phi Delta Kappan 73*(1): 17–27.

Sheingold, K., and M. S. Tucker, eds. 1990. *Restructuring for learning with technology.* New York: Center for Technology in Education and the National Center on Education and the Economy.

Shepard, L. A. 1991. Psychometricians' beliefs about learning. *Educational Researcher 20*(7): 2–11.

Sherry, M. 1990a. Implementing an integrated instructional system: Critical issues. *Phi Delta Kappan 72*(2): 118–20.

———. 1990b. Integrated learning systems: An EPIE institute report: Integrated instructional systems. *T.H.E. Journal 18*(2): 86–89.

———. 1991. The future of integrated learning systems. *Inventing Tomorrow's Schools 1*(1): 6.

———. 1992a. Integrated learning systems: What may we expect in the future? *Educational Technology 32*(9): 58–59.

———. 1992b. How much does an ILS cost? *Electronic Learning 11*(6): 8.

Shockley, H. A. 1992. Turkey or turnkey? Integrating an integrated learning system, *Educational Technology 32*(9): 22–25.

Shore, A., and M. F. Johnson. 1992. Integrated learning systems: A vision for the future. *Educational Technology 32*(9): 36–39.

Sizer, T. R. 1991. No pain, no gain. *Educational Leadership 48*(8): 32–34.

———. 1992a. The bigger picture: Setting high standards with the help of technology. *Electronic Learning 12(2)*: 50.

———. 1992b. Diverse practice, shared ideas: The essential school. In *Organizing for learning: Toward the 21st century,* edited by J. J. Walberg, and J. J. Lane. Reston, VA: National Association of Secondary School Principals.

———. 1992c. *Horace's school: Redesigning the American high school.* New York: Houghton Mifflin.

Slavin, R. E. 1983. *Cooperative learning.* New York: Longman Inc.

———. 1989a. PET and the pendulum: Faddism in education and how to stop it. *Phi Delta Kappan 70*(10): 752–58.

———. 1989b. Reading effects of IBM's "Writing to Read" program: A review of evaluations. *Education, Evaluation and Policy Analysis 13*(1): 1–11.

———. 1993. The student maestro. *Electronic Learning 13*(1): 24–25.

Southwest Plains Regional Service Center. 1989. 2-Way visually interactive instructional television network. Topeka: Paper presented at the Kansas Association of School Boards Technology in Education Conference.

Spiro, R. J., and J. C. Jehng. 1990. Cognitive flexibility and hypertext: Theory and technology for nonlinear and multidimensional transversal of complex subject matter. In *Cognition, education and multimedia: Exploring ideas in high technology,* edited by D. Nix and R. J. Spiro. Hillsdale, NJ: Lawrence Erlbaum Associates.

St. Clair, R. 1989. An information age school. In *Organizing for learning: Toward the 21st century,* edited by H. J. Walberg and J. J. Lane. Reston, VA: National Association of Secondary School Principals.

Stanton, M., and W. Wilson. 1992. Making the most of cable television technology. *T.H.E. Journal 19*(10): 66–68.

Steller, A. 1989. One model for effective educational reform. In *Organizing for learning: Towards the 21st century*, edited by H. J. Walberg and J. J. Lane. Reston, VA: National Association of Secondary School Principals.

Sterns, H. S. 1993. History comes alive. *Electronic Learning* Special Editions: 8–9.

Taylor, J. 1992. Safeguarding computer equipment. "The electronic school," supplement to the *American School Board Journal 178*(9): A27–A34.

Tiene, D. 1993. Channel one: Good or bad news for our schools? *Educational Leadership 50*(8): 46–51.

Toffler, A. 1970. *Future shock*. New York: Random House.

———. 1980. *Third wave*. New York: William Morrow.

———. 1990. *Power shift: Knowledge, wealth and violence at the edge of the 21st century*. New York: Bantam Books

Traub, D. C. 1991. Simulated world as classroom: The potential for designed learning within virtual environments. In *Virtual reality: Theory, practice and promise*, edited by S. K. Helsel and J. P. Roth. Westport, CT: Meckler.

Trotter, A. 1990. Computer Learning. *American School Board Journal 177*(7): 12–18.

———. 1991. Are today's kids having too much fun in your classrooms? *Executive Educator 13*(6): 20–24.

———. 1990. Buying trouble. *American School Board Journal 177*(7): 16–18.

Tucker, M. 1992. The genie in the bottle. *Electronic Learning 12*(3): 50.

Tyre, T. 1992. Jostens learning interactive media: The ultimate ILS delivers networked video. *T.H.E. Journal 20*(1): 14–15.

Tyson, H., and A. Woodward. 1989. Why students aren't learning very much from textbooks. *Educational Leadership 47*(3): 14–17.

U. S. Congress, Office of Technology Assessment. 1988. *Power on!: New tools for teaching and learning*. Washington, DC: U.S. Government Printing Office.

———. 1989. *Linking for learning: A new course for education*. Washington, DC: U.S. Government Printing Office.

U. S. Department of Labor: Secretary's Commission on Achieving Necessary Skills. 1991. *What work requires of schools: A SCANS report on America 2000*. Washington, DC: U. S. Government Printing Office.

Van Dam, A. 1988. Hypertext '87 keynote address. *Comm. ACM 31*(7): 887–95.

Van Den Brink, J. 1994. Outside, a world goes by . . . applying mathematics with flight simulators. *The Computing Teachers 21*(5): 21–32.

Van Dusen, L. M., and B. R. Worthen. 1992. Factors that facilitate or impede implementation of integrated learning systems. *Educational Technology 32*(9): 16–21.

Van Horn, R. 1991. Educational power tools: New instructional delivery systems. *Phi Delta Kappan 72*(7): 527–33.

Vandergrif, K. E., M. Kemper, S. Champion, and J. A. Hannigan. 1987. CD-ROM: An emerging technology: Part 2: Planning and management strategies. *School Library Journal*: 22–25.

Walberg, H. J., and J. J. Lane, eds. 1989. *Organizing for learning: Toward the 21st century.* Reston, VA: National Association of Secondary School Principals.

Ward, A. 1991. Restructuring elementary education. Special supplement to the *Executive Educator 13*(10): A24–A25.

———. 1991. What place does technology deserve in education? Special supplement to the *Executive Educator*.

———. 1992. A brave new information world. "The electronic school," supplement to the *American School Board Journal 178*(9): A16–A18.

Weisberg, L. 1992. Beyond drills & practice in a one computer classroom. *The Computing Teacher 20*(1): 27–28.

Whisler, J. S. 1988. Distance learning technologies: An aid to restructuring schools. In *Noteworthy*, Mid-Continent Regional Educational Laboratory. Washington, DC: U.S. Government Printing Office.

White, M. A. 1986. Implication of the technologies for human learning. *Peabody Journal of Education 64*(1): 155–69.

———. 1987. Information and imagery education. In *What curriculum for the information age?*, edited by M. A. White. Hillsdale, NJ: Lawrence Erlbaum.

———. 1989a. Current trends in education and technology as signs to the future. *Education & Computing 5:* 3–10.

———. 1989b. Educators must ask themselves some important questions. *Electronic Learning 9*(1): 6–8.

———. 1991. Images foster greater learning. *Electronic Learning 11*(1): 6.

———. 1992. Are ILSs good education? *Educational Technology 32*(9): 49–50.

———, ed. 1983. *The future of electronic learning.* Hillsdale, NJ: Lawrence Erlbaum Associates.

———, ed. 1987. *What curriculum for the information age?* Hillsdale, NJ: Lawrence Erlbaum Associates.

Wigley, G. 1988. Telecommunications in the classroom: Telecommunications planning guide for educators. *The Computing Teacher 16(*3): 24–29.

Wilder, G. Z., and M. Fowles. 1992. Assessing the outcomes of computer-based instruction: The experience of Maryland. *T.H.E. Journal 20*(2): 82–84.

Wilson, J. 1990. Integrated learning systems: A primer. *Classroom Computer Learning 10*(5): 22–36.

Wilson, T. 1991. Here's what's on the school technology horizon. Special supplement to *Executive Educator 13(10)*: A11–A13.

Wolf, G. 1995. The curse of Xanadu. *Wired 3*(6): 138–52.

Wood, C., and R. Melville. 1992. Consumer watch: National guide to user groups. *PC World 10*(10): 31–44.

Zorfass, J., and A. R. Remz. 1992. Successful technology integration: The role of communication and collaboration. *Middle School Journal 23*(5): 39–43.

INDEX

Learn from Our Books *and* from Our Authors!

Bring Our Author/Trainers to Your District

At IRI/SkyLight, we have assembled a unique team of outstanding author/trainers with international reputations for quality work. Each has designed high-impact programs that translate powerful new research into successful learning strategies for every student. We design each program to fit your school's or district's special needs.

Training Programs

IRI/SkyLight's training programs extend the renewal process by helping educators move from content-centered to mind-centered classrooms. In our highly interactive workshops, participants learn foundational, research-based information and teaching strategies in an instructional area that they can immediately transfer to the classroom setting. With IRI/SkyLight's specially prepared materials, participants learn how to teach their students to learn for a lifetime.

Network for Systemic Change

Through a partnership with Phi Delta Kappa, IRI/SkyLight offers a Network for site-based systemic change: *The Network of Mindful Schools.* The Network is designed to promote systemic school change as possible and practical when starting with a renewed vision that centers on *what* and *how* each student learns. To help accomplish this goal, Network consultants work with member schools to develop an annual tactical plan and then implement that plan at the classroom level.

Training of Trainers

The Training of Trainers programs train your best teachers, those who provide the highest quality instruction, to coach other teachers. This not only increases the number of teachers you can afford to train in each program, but also increases the amount of coaching and follow-up that each teacher can receive from a resident expert. Our Training of Trainers programs will help you make a systemic improvement in your staff development program.

To receive a FREE COPY of the IRI/SkyLight catalog or more information about trainings offered through IRI/SkyLight, contact CLIENT SERVICES at

TRAINING AND PUBLISHING, INC.
2626 S. Clearbrook Dr., Arlington Heights, IL 60005
800-348-4474 • 847-290-6600 • FAX 847-290-6609

There are

one-story intellects,

two-story intellects, and three-story

intellects with skylights. All fact collectors, who

have no aim beyond their facts, are one-story men. Two-story men

compare, reason, generalize, using the labors of the fact collectors as

well as their own. Three-story men idealize, imagine,

predict—their best illumination comes from

above, through the skylight.

—Oliver Wendell

Holmes

(IRI) SkyLight

TRAINING AND PUBLISHING, INC.